Photographing

BIRDS

IN THE WILD

Photographing BIRDS
IN THE WILD

PHOTOGRAPHS AND TEXT BY

Paul Hicks

PHOTOGRAPHS BY

Russell Hartwell
Malcolm Freeman

DESIGNED BY GRANT BRADFORD

FOUNTAIN PRESS

To my parents for their help
and encouragement. – P.H.

Published by
FOUNTAIN PRESS LIMITED
Fountain House
2 Gladstone Road
Kingston-upon-Thames
Surrey KT1 3HD

© COPYRIGHT
FOUNTAIN PRESS 1999

Text
PAUL HICKS

Photographs
RUSSELL HARTWELL
MALCOLM FREEMAN
PAUL HICKS

Designed by
GRANT BRADFORD
Design Consultants
Tunbridge Wells
Kent

Colour Origination
HBM Singapore

Printed and Bound
in Italy by *SFERA*

ISBN 0 86343 357 X

CONTENTS

INTRODUCTION

As photographic subjects, wild birds present quite a challenge, mainly because their phenomenal eyesight and (in most cases) acutely cautious nature make them so difficult to approach. However, like any good challenge, bird photography can often be tremendously rewarding, and its popularity is ever increasing. As a result, there is a continual improvement in the standard of work being produced. Far from being just a record of species and behaviour, the best bird photographs are genuinely artful images.

My aim in writing this book has been to provide the less experienced photographer with a practical guide to photographing many different species of wild birds in a variety of situations, ranging from an ordinary back garden to a remote Scottish island. I've assumed that you will be using a 35mm single-lens reflex camera, and most of the illustrations reflect my preference for natural lighting – although basic flash techniques, which are sometimes indispensable, are also covered. As I am a photographer and naturalist, rather than a camera enthusiast, the emphasis is on fieldcraft, sound technique and the photographer's creative input, each of these being more important than the use of high-tech equipment.

Whether you are a knowledgeable birder who wishes to find out more about photography, or whether you have a photographic background but need to know more about fieldcraft and specialist techniques, this book should help you to achieve a higher standard. Above all, I hope it increases your enjoyment of a uniquely rewarding pastime.

Many people have assisted me in completing this book, some by making a material contribution, others simply by offering encouragement. If I tried to thank everyone it would sound like an acceptance speech at the Oscars, and would be even less entertaining. So, I'll confine myself to thanking Harry Ricketts of Fountain Press, for having faith in me and remaining patient; Grant Bradford, for his expert work on the design; Celia Coyne, for correcting the grammatical errors what I wrote; and of course, Russell Hartwell and Malcolm Freeman, for lending me some half-decent bird photographs. Russ and Malcolm are fine photographers and fine friends, so I'm delighted that they agreed to collaborate with me. Their contribution has been invaluable.

Paul Hicks.

HIDES AND HIDE PHOTOGRAPHY

The most basic problem in bird photography is the difficulty of getting close to the subject. Of course, there are some exceptional locations where wild birds are so tolerant that you can simply walk right up to within a few feet of them and begin taking pictures. Given favourable terrain, you can stalk more reluctant subjects; but in most situations, there is no substitute for total concealment, and experienced bird photographers know that the best way to achieve this is to shoot from a hide. While the chapter on field techniques is really the most important part of this book, it seems appropriate to begin by covering the basic principles of hide photography, as these will apply to any field technique that involves the use of a hide. First, let's look at the various types of hide:

TRADITIONAL CANVAS HIDE

The best known commercial design of this type is the durable Jamie Wood 'Fensman'. It's roughly cube shaped, the standard size being about 75cm square and up to 120cm high. It has a tubular aluminium frame, a flap at the rear for access, small viewing windows all round and a 'lens funnel' in the front face. Once in position, it is secured with guy ropes, and you can load the side pockets with stones to keep the material taut so that nothing flaps in the wind. The main drawback with this hide is that it is too small to share with a tripod, chair and spare equipment. (If, like me, you believe in being comfortable while you are taking pictures, I'd recommend the larger 'King Fensman'.) Other problems with the standard design include poor forward visibility, an undersized lens funnel and a tendency for the roof to sag and collect rainwater, but these deficiencies are easily rectified. I've cut a large lens/viewing window in the front of my Fensman, which spans the whole width of the front face. Masked by fine netting, it offers excellent visibility and unrestricted movement for the lens, so the original funnel is now redundant. The roof no longer sags as it is supported by a couple of lengths of flexible plastic plumbing tube, wedged across the frame.

In return for the time you spend on establishing hides, you get the opportunity to photograph shy birds like this grey heron from a really intimate viewpoint.
Just being able to observe the birds this closely makes the effort worthwhile; viewing them from afar through a spotting scope simply doesn't compare!

This hide was originally a large galvanised water tank, approximately 2.5m long and 1.5m deep. We rolled it onto its side so that the open top became the front; then we screwed a large sheet of plywood across this, and cut out the windows and door with a jigsaw. There was ample room inside for two photographers and a couple of deckchairs, but it was never very portable!

DOME HIDES

There are several more modern commercial hides that are based on the dome tent principle, whereby the nylon skin is supported and tensioned by a frame of flexible fibreglass rods. This makes the hide more portable and easier to erect, and there is no loose material to flap in the wind and alarm your quarry. The main disadvantage with these hides is that they tend to be expensive. (Bear in mind that even in a seemingly remote corner of the countryside, an unoccupied hide is at risk of theft and vandalism.)

WOODEN HIDES

Unfortunately, the only wooden hide currently available is the one you build yourself. You don't need great carpentry expertise to build a wooden hide (which in my case is just as well!) but you will need to spend a fair amount of time on its construction. In my opinion this is time well spent, because a well made wooden hide will last for years. Another great advantage is that being a solid structure, it won't flap or rock in a strong wind. Since you are the designer, it can also be tailored to your needs.

The simplest form of wooden hide is the non-portable variety, constructed around four sturdy cornerposts. All you do is hammer the posts into the ground, and nail or screw four sheets of plywood to these to form the front, back and sides. A fifth sheet forms the roof. To complete the hide, make a door in the rear panel, cut out a lens window in the front and paint it.

Russell's home-made wooden hide in position on the shore of a Scottish sea loch. Thanks to the rubber skirt, it can be partially submerged at high tide without coming to any harm. On this occasion though, with high winds forecast, we built a small breakwater in front of it to minimise the impact of the waves. It was also very strongly guyed. Construction details for this hide are given overleaf.

Building a portable wooden hide is more complicated. First, I'll admit I use the term 'portable' quite loosely. Wood is a heavy material, and you need a lot of it to build a hide. Even though mine breaks down into ten reasonably manageable pieces. I normally have to carry it in three trips, so it's only suitable for locations that are within easy walking distance of a road. It's basically a wooden box strengthened by an angle-iron frame. The design shown incorporates an unusual refinement devised by Russell Hartwell. He required a hide that could be left in position just below the high water mark on the shore of a sea loch in Islay. The problem was that at high tide, the hide would be standing in 30cm of water. Unable to envisage a portable structure strong enough to resist the combined effect of wind and waves, he devised the 'rubber skirt'. Consisting of strips of rubber cut from old car mats and stapled to wooden battens, the skirt fits around the base of the hide, filling the gap between the wooden sides and the ground. It conceals the occupant's legs and feet, but offers little resistance to the waves when the hide is partially submerged, so the sea just washes through without causing any damage. And it really works; the hide has been left in position for days at a time, surviving successive high tides, even when battered by 90km/h winds.

The diagram shows the finer points of the hide's construction, but I should mention that the frame can be formed from wooden battens rather than steel angle, should you find the latter difficult to obtain or work with – and of course, if you intend to use the hide on dry land only, you can dispense with the rubber skirt. This will

BUILDING A HIDE

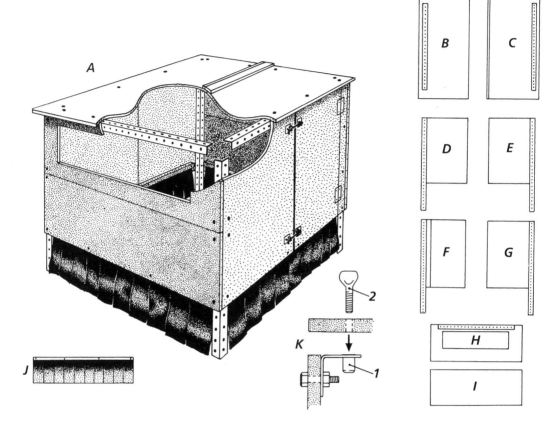

A – Cutaway diagram of main assembly

B – Roof panel, 120cm x 60cm. Dexion 100cm, bolted on 6cm from edge.

C – Roof panel, 120cm x 60cm. Dexion as per B. An additional strip of ply is tacked and glued so as to overlap the centre joint when the two halves are in position.

D – Side panel (closed side), 80cm x 55cm. Dexion 120cm, bolted flush with long edge.

E – Side panel (closed side). Dimensions and dexion as per D.

F – Side panel (door). Overall size 80cm x 55cm, but consists of two pieces joined with hinges; one is 80cm x 10cm - bolt dexion, 120cm, to this piece. The other piece (the door itself) is 80cm x 45cm.

G – Side panel (door side) 80cm x 55cm. Dexion 120cm, flush with long edge.

H – Upper front/rear panel, 110cm x 40cm. Dexion, 100cm bolted flush with top edge. Camera port approx 70cm x 25cm, cut with jigsaw.

I – Lower front/rear panel, 110cm x 40cm.

J – Section of 'Rubber skirt' (1 of 4). Consists of 40cm X 10cm (approx) strips of thick rubber, linoleum or similar material, stapled to a 100cm length of 3cm (11/4 inch) square section wooden batten. Each batten is drilled in four positions and bolted to inside bottom edge of one side of hide.

K – Cross section showing method of joining panels. Dexion frame is drilled and fitted with an M6 nutsert (1). M6 thumbscrew (2) passes through adjoining panel and screws into nutsert.

This hide was designed for use in the tidal zones of estuaries and sea lochs. It can withstand being partially submerged at high tide, because the wooden structure stands clear of the water on stilts. Provided the water is no deeper than 30cm or so, the hide is unaffected by wave action; the sea just washes through the rubber skirt underneath. The basic material is 9mm plywood. Ideally marine ply should be used, but cheaper 'all weather' ply can be used if treated with preservative and sealer prior to painting. The frame is made from lengths of dexion (steel shelving supports) bought secondhand from a supplier of industrial storage products. If you find dexion difficult to obtain or work with, 3cm (11/4 inch) square section wooden batten makes an adequate substitute. For portability (of a kind!) the hide breaks down into 14 pieces. The door opens from the side, and there are large camera ports front and rear. These are shuttered, and fine netting is pinned across whichever one is being used, so as to conceal the photographer. if desired, additional camera ports and/or small viewing windows can be cut in the sides. The dimensions given are for a hide approximately 110cm wide, 110cm long and 120cm high.

N.B. Despite the substantial weight of the assembled hide, it must be securely guyed. Steel eye bolts can be fitted close to the corner of each roof panel to provide secure anchor points for guy ropes.

simplify the construction, but the wooden panels must be enlarged so there is no appreciable gap between the sides of the hide and the ground.

HIDE BUILDING WITH SCRAP MATERIALS

A cheap, serviceable hide can be made from scrap materials, such as old carpet off-cuts, tarpaulins, corrugated iron or whatever else comes to hand. You can't really make a portable hide from these materials, but if you have a long-term project in mind, this is the ideal way to build a hide that will not be stolen, nor represent much of a loss should it be vandalised. As with the more basic wooden hide previously described, you should start by constructing a frame. Typically this could be four posts hammered into the ground, with horizontal battens nailed across the top. The skin of the hide is then draped over and nailed to the frame. The result is unlikely to be very picturesque, but as long as you can see out, and nothing can see in, the hide will do its job.

It's also possible to build mainly with natural materials. The walls can be built with rocks or dead tree branches, while a tarpaulin, supported by a few lengths of wood and weighted down at the edges, makes a good waterproof and lightproof roof. Such a hide should blend well with its surroundings, and since most of the construction materials are gathered locally, you can build at a remote location without having to make repeated hikes laden with wood and tools.

CAMOUFLAGE

First, don't imagine that every hide must be invisible or even inconspicuous. Usually, it's enough that it simply conceals you. Most birds will disregard even a blatantly obvious hide once they have had a few days to get used to it. However, if you are photographing raptors, waders, members of the crow family, or any other particularly wary species, the less conspicuous the hide, the better. Similarly, if time is pressing and photography must begin soon after the hide is in position, camouflage will improve your chances with any species. The hide may also need to be hidden from people, so that it isn't found and interfered with. The obvious problems are, as I've mentioned, theft and vandalism, but worse can happen. I know of one instance where a photographer's hide was discovered by a particularly spiteful individual who waited inside, then shot and killed a kingfisher which settled on a nearby perch.

The quickest way to conceal a hide is to cover it with camouflage netting, which must be stretched taut and pegged down so that it can't flap in the wind. Sprigs of foliage and fistfuls of long grass may then be woven into the netting, so as to break up the hide's outline and help it blend into its surroundings. If you are undertaking a long-term project, you can actually transplant living vegetation, which will grow up to form a natural screen. This is one of Russell's favourite techniques. He begins new hide projects early in the year, and provided the surrounding area is not unduly sensitive, he supplements existing natural cover with plenty of young bushes, dug up from nearby and replanted around his hide. By midsummer, these have sprouted forth to render the hide undetectable in the midst of its own little thicket.

Although this blue tit appears to have perched on a barbed wire fence, it's actually on a prop. The post was hammered into the ground a few feet in front of the hide, and screwed to the back of it, hidden from the lens, was a peanut feeder. The barbed wire ended in mid-air just a few centimetres to the right of the bird. And they say the camera never lies! It's actually the most convincing liar of all. 300mm lens with x1.4 teleconverter.

CHOOSING A LOCATION

While I can't give specific advice on where to locate your hide, there are some basic points which apply anywhere. The most obvious requirement is that the hide must provide an intimate and unobstructed view of the subject, but don't neglect other factors such as lighting and background. I'm so fussy about lighting that if I have to set up a hide in overcast weather, I use a compass to confirm

The 'fake' fencepost from behind, revealing peanut feeder and hide beyond.

where the sun will rise and set. This gives me a fair idea of how the subject will be illuminated under a clear sky. I also look for potential eyesores in the background, bearing in mind that, once I am in the hide, I won't be able to change my viewpoint. In hide photography, thorough preparation is the key to success.

USING A HIDE

The hide will only be effective if it is used properly. Depending on the species and circumstances in question, your preparatory work may be in vain if you make an incautious entry or exit, or if you behave carelessly whilst inside. It's true that some birds will tolerate a fairly lax approach by the photographer. For example, many garden birds will perch on a hide within hours of it being erected. You can enter in full view, and within a few minutes, they'll be back. Noises from within the hide are largely ignored, and even quite obvious movements of the lens may not cause alarm. However, in most situations, great care must be employed. First, you must enter the hide without being seen. Some birds will watch from afar as you approach the hide, and having seen you go inside, they will remain wary. Even hours later, the hide will be treated with suspicion, unless you have been seen to emerge and leave. The best solution is to approach with a companion, who departs once you are inside. Theoretically any bird that happens to be watching will note the departure of your accomplice, decide that the danger has passed, and happily approach the hide. This technique normally works well, thanks to the birds' somewhat limited mathematical and deductive skills. (The phrase, 'bird brain' wasn't coined for nothing!) However, some species can count better than others. Expert opinion has it that sometimes, three or four accomplices are required before the deception will work. (As far as I am concerned, the question is academic, as I've never been able to find more than one person obliging enough – or daft enough – to get up before dawn and hike out to one of my hides.) What if no accomplice is available? The next best thing is to arrive in darkness and make a discreet approach. Even in darkness, the upright human form is easily recognised, so cross open ground on all fours and show your face as little as possible.

Once you are inside the hide get everything ready immediately, even if you aren't expecting any action for a while. The tripod should be level, so that you can maintain a level horizon while panning, and the front of the lens hood should protrude no more than 3 – 4cm beyond the net screen. (Birds will be less wary of the lens if you leave a dummy lens in position whenever the hide is unoccupied. Nothing fancy is required; a black flowerpot will do.) Next, fresh rolls of film, accessories, food and drink etc., should be laid out close to hand, so you don't have to waste time or make a noise looking for them later, when there might be a nervous subject just a few metres away. Remain inside the hide for the duration of the session, and avoid making any noises which might cause alarm. Above all, when you have to move the lens, move it very slowly, and only when your subject is looking away. Nothing is more likely to put a bird to flight than a sudden, careless movement of the lens. Finally, when leaving the hide, employ the same caution as when entering. Have your accomplice walk out to the hide to meet you, or leave in darkness.

There is one rarely mentioned problem which inevitably arises during any long hide session. Namely, how to answer the call of nature without going outside. My solution is borrowed from the army – I use plastic bags, which can be sealed and disposed of later. Well, nobody said hide photography was glamorous...

This yellowhammer perched so close to Malcolm's hide that he could barely fit it into the frame. We often included this shot in presentations for camera clubs and naturalist groups, because when projected, its sheer size and the minute feather detail always made a big impression on the audience. Between the three of us it became known as "The Attack of the Fifty-Foot Yellowhammer!"

FIELD TECHNIQUES

PHOTOGRAPHING SMALL BIRDS
AT A FEEDING STATION

Anyone with an interest in birds will know how easy it is to attract many garden and woodland species with food. Food can, of course, be used to attract birds to a hide, and if the supply is maintained over a long period, birds which visit regularly will lose much of their natural caution. Before long, the hide is ignored (or used as a convenient perch!) and it becomes possible to photograph from very close range, so you can shoot portraits with a 300mm or even 200mm lens. This is the ideal technique to use in a garden, even in urban surroundings, because comparatively little space is required and most garden birds respond readily to any offer of food. It also works well in rural areas, particularly in the vicinity of hedgerows and woodland edges.

It's essential to maintain a constant food supply over a long period. Although some species will take advantage of new food sources within minutes, several weeks or even months may elapse before the number and variety of visitors reaches its peak. To encourage a variety of birds, offer a variety of foods, and present them in different ways. I normally put out two or three hanging feeders containing nuts and seed, plus a large, home-made, fatty seed cake. On the ground, there should be a liberal scattering of mixed seed and other loose food items such as fruit, bread and scraps from the table. Finally, don't forget a shallow pool for drinking and bathing.

Not every shot has to exclude the feeders. As far as the birds are concerned, they're just another part of the environment, and of course they are the focus of much interesting activity. Here a house sparrow has ousted the usual assortment of tits to grab an easy meal.
500mm lens with 27.5mm extension tube.

Peanuts are one of the most nutritious birdfoods and they have a broad appeal. In gardens, they usually attract an assortment of tits and finches, but if there is any woodland nearby, nuthatches, great spotted woodpeckers and jays may appear. Whole peanuts can choke young birds, so they should be presented in wire mesh feeders, which ensure that the birds can only extract fragments. A feeder also limits the number of birds that can feed at any one time. From the photographer's point of view, this is a distinct advantage, because excellent photo opportunities occur when birds that are awaiting their turn to feed 'queue up'

on nearby perches. Feeder designs are many and varied. The cheapest is the red plastic net bag, whose unique advantage over other feeders is that it may attract siskins. For some reason, these birds will rarely take peanuts from anything else. However, red bags allow birds to take whole nuts, and are hopelessly vulnerable to attack by squirrels. A more robust alternative is the basic wire mesh tube, but these will fail if subjected to a really determined assault by 'educated' squirrels. Squirrel-proof designs include stainless steel versions of the basic mesh tube, ceramic feeders, and caged feeders, which are protected by steel bars set just wide enough to admit small birds, while excluding squirrels .

Peanuts can be used to set up shots of birds appearing to feed naturally. When concealed in crevices in coarse tree bark they will attract great spotted woodpeckers and nuthatches, which can then be photographed apparently probing for beetle larvae! You can also cram them into specially drilled holes to achieve the same result. When offered in this way, they still attract tits and finches, who, being first on the scene, may clean out the holes before anything else gets a look in. If this becomes a problem, deepen the holes slightly to put the nuts just beyond their reach. You could also try crushing peanuts and offering

In order to attract a broad range of species, offer a variety of foods and present them in different ways. This brambling was attracted by mixed seed, scattered loose on the ground. 300mm lens with x1.6 teleconverter.

Great spotted woodpeckers can't resist the lure of peanuts. To obtain authentic looking shots like this (as opposed to pictures of birds on feeders) prop up a dead bough, and drill a dozen or so holes in one side. These should be about 10mm in diameter and about 25mm deep. Cram peanuts into the holes, crushing them right in with the blunt end of a pencil, so that the birds cannot extract whole nuts. Woodpeckers (and nuthatches) will cling to the perch for minutes at a time, pecking away as if digging out grubs. 500mm lens.

them loose, either on the ground or on a bird table. This may attract species that do not like whole nuts, treecreepers being a notable example.

Another popular birdfood is 'wild bird seed'. Its quality and content is variable, so beware of unmarked bags containing a high percentage of dried vegetable matter and unidentifiable tat. The better brand-name seed contains a good mix of quality grains, and when scattered on the ground as a loose feed, it attracts a fair variety of birds, including some which will not visit hanging feeders, such as yellowhammers and bramblings. If there is woodland nearby, wood pigeons and pheasants may appear, the latter being a mixed blessing due to their phenomenal appetite.

Two kinds of sunflower seed are sold as wild bird foods. The standard black-and-white striped variety is the more familiar, as it is sold by most pet stores and garden centres, but recently, black sunflower seed has become popular. Specialist suppliers claim that it is the most effective single seed you can offer. Certainly, finches in particular will besiege any feeder containing it, while ignoring adjacent feeders containing mixed seed. Black sunflower complements peanuts perfectly, as it attracts a different

Fieldfares are one of several species which can be attracted with fruit. While it's usually a good idea to exclude any signs of 'bait', for this shot Russell chose to make the apples an important part of the picture, piling them up to fill the foreground. The unusual result is far more appealing than the obvious 'bird on lawn' shot. 500mm lens.

Because the female greenfinch and its background looked rather drab, Malcolm incorporated the rosehips into his set up to add some colour.
This approach can be taken further – in fact, when some form of bait is used, it's possible to lure many garden birds into what is virtually an outdoor studio, complete with 'prop' perches and artificial backdrop. 300mm lens with x1.6 teleconverter.

range of species, and individual seeds are easy to conceal, should you wish to simulate 'natural' feeding behaviour. For example, you can insert them into dead teasel heads to attract goldfinches, which can then be photographed feeding 'naturally'. While black sunflower is supposedly the ultimate seed, in my experience the old fashioned stripy stuff runs it a close second, and is well worth trying.

Fruit is an excellent offering, especially in early winter. Old apples or pears can be scattered on the ground or placed among tree branches to attract birds that have little or no interest in nuts and seed, such as redwings, fieldfares, blackbirds, thrushes, and even green woodpeckers. Live foods are popular throughout the year, and especially so during the breeding season. A cheap and simple way of providing live foods is to build up a compost heap, which will soon become infested with worms and insects.

23

This is another example of how effective the right combination of bait and a well established hide can be. The fieldfare had been attracted by a scattering of old apples, and remained relaxed in a nearby hedgerow, only a few feet in front of Russell's hide. Of course, great care is still required; at such close range, even minor movements of the lens will cause alarm.
400mm lens with 27.5mm extension tube.

Alternatively, mealworms and waxworms (actually types of beetle larvae) can be purchased from specialist suppliers and some pet stores. While robins are happy to take these from an open dish, wrens, being accustomed to finding food among dense cover, may need some encouragement. Try partially covering the food dish; this seems to tempt them to explore the dark interior.

If you provide water at the feeding station, birds will come to drink and bathe, especially during prolonged dry spells and in cold winter weather when natural sources freeze. Because the appeal of water is universal, it may attract birds that cannot be tempted with food. An upturned dustbin lid, propped up on bricks, makes an excellent pool. as it holds a reasonable quantity of water but is not too deep. If you wish to photograph the birds as they bathe or drink, you can build and landscape a small pool; this makes

It's hard to imagine a picture that could better convey the bitter chill of midwinter than this portrait of a yellowhammer in frost. For a week or so in late December, Buckinghamshire was shrouded in freezing fog, and the rime frost grew thicker by the day. A well-maintained feeding station gave Malcolm a ready supply of subjects, but the poor light and intense cold made photography difficult. This shot proved the value of perseverance, and was highly commended in the Wildlife Photographer of the Year Competition. 300mm lens with x1.6 teleconverter.

a more pleasing backdrop. The pool's allure will be improved if there is dripping water, which many birds seem to find irresistible.

Although a feeding station can provide photo opportunities throughout the year, the activity will peak during the winter and early spring, especially during spells of cold weather. Autumn is therefore the ideal time to get a project of this kind underway. Maintaining the feeding station through the winter requires a certain amount of commitment, because some birds will become dependent on it, and they may starve if you suddenly abandon it when natural foods are scarce. Putting food out in your own garden involves little or no inconvenience, but don't choose a more distant location unless you are sure that you can make regular visits in all weathers. The financial outlay on birdfood is another consideration. This should not prove prohibitive, particularly if you buy in bulk at the outset, but progressively more food will be required as an ever-increasing number of birds come to feed.

Ideally a feeding station should be sited close to a natural feature that is already favoured by the birds, such as a hedge or treeline. Natural cover provides small birds with a refuge against attack by raptors, so they are more relaxed, perching for long periods and singing more readily. The photographic potential here is obvious, but to make the most of it, you must employ a little subtlety. Don't place the feeders within such a refuge, otherwise it will be disturbed by the melee which develops around them. The only photo opportunities will be fleeting ones, as birds flit to and fro between the feeders and engage in minor hierarchical disputes. If you are trying to photograph birds in say, a hedgerow, it's best to put the feed in the open, several metres away. (If there is nothing to hang the feeders from, mount them on posts.) A steady traffic will develop between the feed and the closest point of the hedgerow, so position the hide to overlook this area. At times, birds will virtually line up along the branches, some waiting to feed, others simply resting and even dozing .

Maximise the photographic potential of your chosen location by introducing natural and artificial props. For example, you could lure birds on to a gnarled, lichen encrusted bough, carefully placed against a pleasing background. Alternatively, a dead treestump could be drilled and stuffed with peanuts to attract woodpeckers. As an alternative to the inevitable 'bird on twig' shot, set up a man-made perch such as a fence post, or a piece of garden or farm machinery. Usually the best way to lure birds on to a prop is to place it between the feeders and whatever cover they are using, so that it becomes an intermediate stop for birds that are about to feed. Don't expect a bird to relax on an exposed perch; it will pause only briefly, remaining fully alert and constantly looking around for danger, so your shots must be timed to catch the brief moments when it is suitably posed.

Part of the appeal of photographing birds at a feeding station is that many of the regular visitors become remarkably bold, remaining close by while you top up the feeders, and returning to feed within seconds once you have entered the hide. Even shy species are quick to appear when encouraged by the sight of a mob of blue tits and greenfinches happily tucking in to a free meal. So, while you should always behave discreetly while you are inside the hide, don't worry too much if you can't conceal your arrival and departure.

Common Buzzard. It's a good idea to set up a prominent perch close to a carrion bait. If it is used, you should have an excellent opportunity to shoot some portraits which are reasonably free of gore.
600mm lens.

BAITING WITH CARRION

Food, this time in the form of carrion. (i.e. dead rabbits, pheasants, pigeons and even butcher's scraps) can be used to attract various members of the crow family, some of the larger gulls, and raptors, including buzzards, red kites, hen harriers and even golden eagles. If you live outside the range of some of these birds you'll be unable to establish a long-term feeding station for them. However, while regular baiting over an extended period is the most effective approach, short-term projects can also succeed, and this technique is well worth trying during a field trip of three or four days duration.

The location of the hide is critical to success with corvids and raptors, because persecution by man has made these birds extremely wary. Any potential source of human disturbance should be given a wide berth, so avoid roads, public footpaths and farm buildings. Ideally, you should set up on land where there is no public access, or failing that, find a location that is remote enough to make human intrusion unlikely.

Once you have access to a suitable area, the next step is to place the bait where it has the best chance of being found. In unfamiliar territory, make use of local knowledge. Advice from a sympathetic landowner or gamekeeper (they do exist!) is invaluable. In the absence of such advice, you must devote plenty of time to observation. You may notice, for example, that a certain telegraph pole or treetop is often occupied by a buzzard or raven. These birds invariably have favourite perches from which they regularly survey their territory, and a bait placed within plain view of such a well-used vantage point will not go unnoticed for long. Alternatively, look for areas which are rich in prey species. Raptors concentrate on these areas when they are hunting. For example, buzzards and hen harriers routinely work low along hedgerows and grassy banks, hoping to ambush rabbits feeding nearby. One note of caution: beware of prey species which gang up! Ground nesting gulls and waders fall into this category, as they mob raptors and corvids relentlessly. I once set up near a mixed colony of common gull, redshank and curlew, in the mistaken belief that this would be the first stop for every hungry predator and nest-robber in the area. My first (and only) session in that hide was an education as every raptor, raven and crow that came up the pike was immediately driven off by a hysterical mob. One buzzard eventually managed to land beside the bait, but despite his obviously benign intentions, he was mercilessly dive-bombed and soon followed on the heels of earlier visitors. Since that day, I've never tried this approach near a nest colony.

The bait should be as conspicuous as possible when viewed from the air. One reason why rabbits make good baits is that, when laid out belly up, the white underside can be seen from afar. Gruesome though it may be, the appeal of a carcass will be further enhanced if it is cut open to expose the entrails. While raptors are usually happy to do their own butchery, gulls and members of the crow family like to be able to tuck straight in to a beakfull of tender giblets. Make things easy for them, because when they are confronted with an intact carcass, they will sometimes give it a couple of half-hearted pecks and then fly away. The bait should also be pegged down, because given the

Hen Harriers are normally reluctant to take carrion, but this female was one of a pair who repeatedly visited our baits during cold weather in February. They were ravenous, each bird staying for up to an hour at a time.
500mm lens.

chance, a raptor will simply pick up a rabbit or pigeon and fly off with it, rather than feed in front of the hide. Gulls and crows, while unable to fly with adult rabbits, will still drag them away from the hide. Secure two of the bait's legs with tent pegs, making sure that the tops of the pegs are not visible in the viewfinder.

To complete the arrangement, I invariably set up a perch close to the bait. An old fencepost or a gnarled bough $1^1/_2$-2m long is ideal. This should be erected to one side of the bait (as viewed from the hide) and a couple of metres further back, so as to provide a reassuringly secure vantage point for birds which might be too cautious to drop straight on to the bait. You'll definitely get more photo opportunities with a perch in place, some of which will be 'bird on post' portraits in addition to the obvious 'bird on carrion' shots. Furthermore, the perch will occasionally attract chance visitors that have no interest in the bait, especially in open country where few other perches are available. You can imagine my delight when, during a winter field trip to Islay, an otherwise bleak and unrewarding day in the hide was transformed by the arrival of a male sparrowhawk, who suddenly materialised on a weathered bough that I had set up for buzzards. He was hunting in earnest. Within seconds there was a sudden, tense crouch as something caught his eye in the

gorse further down the hillside; probably a meadow pipit. Then he launched into the wind and went scything away across the heather, having given me just enough time to shoot three frames.

With the bait and hide in position, there is little to do but leave it and see what happens. Time permitting, I don't attempt any photography until after the bait has been discovered, which sometimes takes a couple of days. I check it at the end of each day, and if I find it partially eaten, I enter the hide before first light the next morning. Although I have known crows and gulls to appear before sunrise, it's best to gird your loins for a long wait, during which time the image framed within the viewfinder will probably become imprinted on your brain! Perhaps because of your restricted vision, you'll also become keenly attuned to the sounds of the landscape, as you strain to hear the thin call of a soaring raptor or the peculiar sound made by curious ravens – like a pebble plopping into a bucket of water. Have faith; eventually, something will happen. You may be forewarned by the heavy beat of unseen wings overhead, but even large raptors can drift in quite soundlessly, so remain alert. When, after a long wait, a bird finally arrives, the effect is electrifying. Stay calm, re-check your exposure setting, and before shooting, take

During a day-long session baiting buzzards in Islay, this male sparrowhawk alighted briefly on the perch. Of course, he was not interested in the rabbit carcass; he was just having a rest while hunting meadow pipits. This incident highlighted the value of having a perch in front of the hide. 500mm lens.

Beautiful but very cold winter weather on Islay. Next to me is a well-camouflaged home-made hide which yielded some useful pictures of buzzards feeding on carrion.

Another portrait taken when a bird settled on a perch that had been set up close to a carrion bait. The magpie is looking around warily before dropping on to the bait.

note of the bird's mood. A relaxed bird will be concentrating on the bait. Shoot a single frame, and if there is no sign of alarm, carry on. After a while, even short bursts of motordrive may be ignored. More caution is required if the bird seems suspicious of the hide. In this case, wait for it to settle down and begin feeding before you shoot the first frame. If it starts at the sound of the camera, allow plenty of time for it to settle again before shooting a second frame. And however confident your subject appears, never move the lens when it is looking your way.

Baiting can succeed at any time of the year, but it is most effective during the autumn and winter, when several factors work in the photographer's favour. Firstly, natural food is harder to come by, the summer glut of eggs, nestlings and young mammals having run out. Immature

After a lengthy programme of baiting, Malcolm began to attract red kites on a daily basis. The birds refused to use a perch that had been set up close to the bait; however, a nearby tree line became a favourite vantage point for them, so Malcolm moved his hide and after a number of fruitless sessions, a kite landed in the right place. So often in bird photography, 'good luck' is really the result of hard work and persistence.
600mm lens with x1.4 teleconverter.

Baiting with carrion works best when natural food is in short supply. This buzzard was photographed during freezing weather in March, when much of its staple diet – ranging from worms and reptiles to lapwing chicks and rabbits – was unavailable or less abundant than at other times in the year.
500mm lens.

raptors and corvids are on the move. These newly independent birds have yet to perfect their hunting skills and are less wary than their parents, so they are more inclined to come down to a bait. Cold weather also helps, because it causes birds to burn more energy and increase their food intake. Hunting activity is further intensified by being compressed into perhaps eight hours of daylight, while the shorter days also make dawn-to-dusk photo sessions more feasible.

ATTRACTING KINGFISHERS

The kingfisher is one of the most beautiful and photogenic of British birds, but obtaining an outstanding picture of one can be difficult, not least because, as a protected species under the Wildlife and Countryside Act, it cannot be photographed near the nest without a Schedule 1 licence. For most photographers, the best chance of success therefore lies in setting up a hide at a good fishing perch, on a stretch of water that is as free from human disturbance as possible. The perch itself need not be an established natural feature, because despite their shyness, kingfishers will readily use a perch that has been put in place by the photographer. This means you have some freedom to to choose your location, provided, of course,

Warm sunlight makes a kingfisher glow against a backdrop of bare branches in mid-winter. Despite its small size, and the busy background, the subject is by far the strongest element in the picture. This is partly a result of careful composition (the kingfisher falling on one of the rule of thirds 'points of power'), and partly because of the subject's bright colour among drab surroundings.
600mm lens.

"Which one next?"
A kingfisher, bathing in rich winter sunlight, peers down into the bait bucket.
500mm lens.

that the perch overlooks good fishing. Now, here's the clever part. You can guarantee good fishing by placing a tub of small live fish under the perch. The fish must be of a suitably authentic species (which rules out a midnight raid on your neighbour's goldfish pond), but catching enough minnows, bullheads etc by hand is difficult and time consuming. Instead, you could enquire at a commercial fish farm. These will often sell live fingerling trout but, if available, coarse fish such as roach and rudd are even better, as they are easier to keep and transport. The bait bucket, weighted with a few inches of gravel, should be placed in shallow water beneath the perch, its rim a few centimetres clear of the water's surface so that the fish cannot escape. Stand it on bricks if the water is too deep. The sides of the bucket should be perforated so that fresh water flows through, and you may need to fit a chicken wire 'funnel' around the rim to deter herons. Be prepared

to re-stock three or four times a week, because once a kingfisher realises that the bucket contains easy pickings, it will take several fish per day. Wait until a bird is visiting regularly before attempting the first photo session and don't automatically assume that if fish are disappearing, a kingfisher must be the culprit. Even if you've managed to exclude herons, mink or grass snakes may be raiding the bucket. Look for the kingfisher's unmistakable calling card: a smattering of tiny fish scales on the perch, dislodged as the bird bludgeons its catch into submission.

Inherent in bird photography are the difficulties of finding, and getting close to, good subjects. When you tire of these difficulties, head for a seabird colony such as this one on the island of Craigleith in the Firth of Forth. Puffins and other seabirds gather here in their thousands, and you certainly won't need a hide!
35-105mm lens.

SEABIRD COLONIES

While only a few of the UK's indigenous birds can match the gaudy plumage of many tropical species, we nevertheless have an avian spectacle to equal almost any in the world, in the form of our teeming seabird colonies. During the breeding season, a variety of birds – notably gannets, puffins, guillemots, razorbills, kittiwakes, shags and terns – gather in huge numbers at key sites around British shores. Among the jabbering hordes, unparalleled photo opportunities are to be had, and because many of these birds show little or no fear of man while breeding, for once you are not shackled by a hide.

Seabird colonies offer excellent opportunities to photograph behaviour such as this gannet courtship.
500mm lens.

Before investing time and money in a field trip to a major seabird colony, make sure that the location you have in mind does offer first class photo opportunities. Some renowned breeding sites are disappointing from a photographic point of view, either because the birds are breeding on inaccessible cliff ledges, or because visitors are barred from large areas to protect vulnerable nests.

I would advise anyone considering their first field trip to play safe and head for either the Farne Islands (off the Northumbrian coast) or the Bass Rock and Craigleith (both in the Firth of Forth). These offer some of the finest seabird photography in Europe. The main drawback where all bird islands are concerned is that they become inaccessible in

This picture was directly inspired by the shot of the fulmar colony. This time, the birds are kittiwakes, and the background is man-made – the crumbling wall of a ruined castle.
The placement of the birds dictated a portrait, rather than landscape format.
As with the fulmars, I tried to time the shot so that something of interest could be seen at each nest – although trying to watch all of the nests at the same time did prove to be impossible!
300mm lens.

bad weather, so it is impossible to plan field trips far in advance. You may also have only a limited amount of time ashore, especially at the Farnes, although the photo opportunities here are good enough to make even a short visit worthwhile.

For most visitors, the sheer spectacle of a major breeding site at the height of the season is unforgettable. Chattering, squabbling birds carpet the ground for hundreds of yards around, and wheel overhead in their thousands. There is photographic potential everywhere you look, and this can be quite bewildering. If you find yourself wondering where to start, my advice would be to leave your camera in its bag until you have had a good look

Although many seabirds will allow a close approach when they are nesting, don't assume that every shot should be a frame filling portrait. Sometimes the wider view is stronger. In this shot of a fulmar colony, all of the birds are rather small in the frame, but several pairs are visible, and something different is going on at each nest. It's a birdy soap opera, being played out against a rather pleasing backdrop of lush grasses and wild flowers. It was a category winner in the 1995 Wildlife Photographer of the Year competition. 300mm lens.

around. Don't rush; accept that you won't be able to photograph everything, and concentrate on making a good job of a few key pictures. When you are assessing possible viewpoints for these, don't let your excitement at finding a terrific subject distract you from basic considerations such as lighting, backgrounds and so on.

One of the joys of photographing a seabird colony is that for once you can get very close and employ a whole range of lenses, including wideangles. With a wideangle lens you can picture the birds against a great sweep of their environment, and the unusually close viewpoint results in some dramatic perspective effects. This type of shot usually works best if both subject and background appear sharp, so maximise the depth of field by setting the smallest lens aperture you can get away with. It's often suggested that because breeding seabirds can be photographed at close quarters, there is no point in carrying super-telephoto lenses, the implication being that these are just for photographing unapproachable subjects. I disagree. With a long lens you can more easily isolate individual birds against a clean background. You can also make images which better portray the sense of overcrowding, as the long lens can fill the frame with a distant section of the

These puffins appealed because they were tightly packed, and the group forms a pleasing curve through the frame. There are no distractions in the background, so all that remained was to sit and wait for them to... be puffins. The little fellow on the left made the shot when he looked back into the frame and yawned. 300mm lens.

This picture is a good example of how, even in a crowded nest colony, it can pay to ignore the hubbub and devote a lot of time to photographing one individual. I spent about an hour with this puffin, during which time I moved progressively closer in order to shoot some intimate portraits.
500mm lens with x1.4 teleconverter and 52.5mm extension tube.

colony where the effect of perspective causes the birds to appear more tightly packed. This is why, on any field trip to a seabird colony, I carry the full range of focal lengths from 24mm wideangle to 500mm telephoto and x1.4 teleconverter.

At any seabird colony there is constant activity, whether it be courtship, the feeding of young, or disputes over territory and food. Unfortunately, when you try to photograph this behaviour, it becomes apparent that at any one nest, brief moments of action punctuate long periods of inactivity. It helps if you can find a viewpoint that gives a clear view of several nests. This is easy if, for example, you are shooting across a gulley at a tight group of nest ledges on a cliff face. However, where the nests are widely spaced, and particularly if they are on the ground, you may have no alternative but to pick one and wait for something to happen.

Seabird colonies also provide marvellous opportunities to photograph birds in flight. Gannets are among the easiest of all subjects for flight photography, thanks to their obliging habit of hanging almost motionless on the breeze. This is best seen at the Bass Rock, where, on a windy day, literally thousands of gannets ride the updraught, the

closest of them drifting past almost within arm's reach of photographers on the walkway. Of course, other species provide a sterner test of your ability, with the smaller, fast flying birds like puffins challenging even the most capable photographer. Specific techniques for action and flight photography are covered later in this chapter.

SHOOTING FROM THE CAR WINDOW

Perhaps surprisingly, birds are quite tolerant of cars, normally showing far less concern at the approach of a vehicle than they would at the sight of a human on foot. A car can therefore serve as a mobile hide, bringing you within range of birds which would otherwise be impossible to photograph.

Before going any further, I should emphasise that when you are shooting from a vehicle, road safety is the overriding consideration. It's easy to become so engrossed in your photography that you become a hazard to yourself and other road users. If you have a 4x4 vehicle and can go off-road, so much the better, but otherwise, reserve this approach for quiet backroads, and don't stop near bends or blind summits. I can vouch for the fact that, though it

One of the joys of working tolerant subjects like these gannets is that, within reason, you can get as close as you like, and employ a whole range of lenses. For this shot I chose a 24mm wideangle. Its terrific field of view allowed me to include a group of birds on the nest, an individual overflying them, and in the background, a great sweep of that gorgeous azure sky.

Right: In most seabird colonies, there is usually plenty of visual interest in the background, which is why many photographers employ wideangle lenses for portraiture. Shots like this are also informative. This one gives the viewer an excellent impression of where and how the shag lives.
35-70mm lens.

This picture is a good example of how, even in a crowded nest colony, it can pay to ignore the hubbub and devote a lot of time to photographing one individual. I spent about an hour with this puffin, during which time I moved progressively closer in order to shoot some intimate portraits. Eventually he decided that I was harmless and began doze off, allowing me the opportunity to make this unusual image.
500mm lens with x1.4 teleconverter and 52.5mm extension tube.

may be 5.30am and apparently the loneliest road in Scotland, if you stop for just a few seconds on a blind bend, a huge tractor, bristling with bits of murderous looking machinery and driven by a white-knuckled maniac, is guaranteed to come roaring around the corner!

Car window photography is best tackled with a really long lens, a focal length of at least 400mm being essential for individual portraits. As always, the lens requires some support. Many photographers favour car window clamps, which enable a tripod head to be fitted to the door or a partially lowered window. These provide solid support, but can't match the faster handling that you get by resting the lens on a beanbag. A beanbag can also be wedged over the

Be prepared to spend some time with a subject to get the best possible result. I edged to within 2.5m of this puffin, who eyed me suspiciously for some time before concluding that I was harmless. For about half an hour, I kept him perfectly framed and in focus, ready for the moment when he would relax and do something interesting. His yawn made the wait well worthwhile.
500mm lens with x1.4 teleconverter and 52.5mm extension tube.

wing mirror, allowing you to lean out a little and shoot almost straight ahead. A beanbag is less convenient when shooting from the driver's seat through the passenger's window, as you must lean awkwardly across to reach the sill, so for passenger-side shooting, I use my Benbo tripod. This is set up across the passenger seat, with two of its legs wedged into the footwell, and the third trapped under the head rest. The tripod is then lashed down with bungees, to prevent it from toppling over when the car is moving. Although this arrangement offers rather a limited field of view, the lens does not protrude from the car so it is less likely to alarm the subject. As a result, it's often possible to pull up directly alongside a bird.

While driving, I leave my camera and 500mm lens mounted on the tripod, with the remote release fitted and correct exposure set, ready for immediate use. The quick release plate allows me to detach the outfit for driver's side shooting at a moment's notice. Various accessories are kept close at hand on the passenger seat, including the beanbag, a shorter lens (usually a 300mm), x1.4 teleconverter, 27.5mm extension tube, and spare film.

The typical car-window 'bird on fencepost'. In terms of composition, these shots work best if the subject is placed high in the frame, so you can see plenty of fencepost. With the bird lower in the frame, the picture would look unbalanced. 500mm lens.

The trick with car window photography is to drive slowly, in order to see potential subjects in good time and make a reasonably discreet approach. When a subject comes into view, stop and check that you are ready to shoot. If you need to swap lenses, check the exposure or wind down the window, do so while you are still some way off. Nervous subjects must be 'stalked' with the vehicle; crawl forward a few metres at a time, stopping repeatedly for a minute or two, so that the bird has time to become accustomed to the car. The critical moment comes when the car is stopped at the desired viewpoint. The engine must then be cut in order to prevent its vibration from causing camera shake, and the sudden silence will often put a nervous bird to flight. (The ideal situation for a successful 'stalk' with the car arises when a subject is seen ahead and can be approached on a downhill slope. It may then be possible to cut the engine well in advance and coast quietly into

A very untypical shot from the car window – a corncrake. Malcolm caught this one skulking in long grass at the roadside. Plenty of focal length was required. 600mm lens with x1.4 teleconverter.

When I was still some way off, I noticed this snipe calling from a post on a fence that ran at ninety degrees to the road. I could see that he was too far from the road for any chance of a portrait, but I thought the fenceline itself had potential. I drove slowly forward and stopped in such a position that the fenceline ran diagonally away from the camera. This meant that only the snipe and his post would appear sharp, so despite his small size within the frame, he still dominates the picture. 500mm lens.

position – but do ensure that your safety is not compromised by a loss of power to the vehicle's steering and braking systems.) Once you are close to a subject, bear in mind that the car doesn't offer the same degree of concealment that you would have in hide. Wear dark gloves and don't show your face. A ski mask can be helpful, although it does attract some funny looks from other motorists.

Car window photography can be rewarding at any time of the year. I use the technique most often during field trips to Scotland. particularly in areas of moorland and marsh, where roadside fenceposts are the most prominent perches available. During the spring and summer a variety of birds, ranging from stonechat to snipe, call from these posts, and being somewhat preoccupied, they are relatively easy to

This shot of a little ringed plover shows that a car can make a very effective hide. There would have been no chance of making such a close approach on foot.
600mm lens.

approach. It's not unusual to set out at first light and be back in time for breakfast having shot several rolls of film. During the autumn and winter, the car is the ideal means of photographing geese as they graze in roadside fields. Hide photography is more successful at roosts, but during the day, when the flocks are moving regularly between feeding grounds, the car's mobility is invaluable.

A HIDE AT THE NEST

Years ago, bird photography was conducted almost exclusively at the nest, mainly because of the constraints imposed by the equipment of the day. Fast super-telephoto lenses were not available, and high quality images could only be made on slow film, so the photographer was often compelled to work at close range with flash. Careful preparation was required, and success depended on the subject returning to a preselected spot, so the nest was by far the best bet. More recently though, there has been a move away from nest photography. The technique has been so widely used that it offers little scope for anyone hoping to produce original images, and modern equipment has freed the photographer to adopt a more imaginative approach and tackle more challenging

situations. Also, there is a growing sense that pressuring birds at the nest is unacceptable. Even with the best of intentions, there is some risk of disturbing the parents or bringing the nest to the attention of a predator, which is why certain species may not be photographed near the nest unless the photographer is licensed by the Nature Conservancy Council in accordance with the Wildlife and Countryside Act 1981, Schedule 1. (Part 1 of the schedule lists those species protected by the act.)

If you decide to try nest photography, the first step is to ensure that the species in question is not protected. Then you must select a suitable nest. Aside from being accessible, it must not be obscured by too much vegetation. A few fronds of foliage can be temporarily tied back while shooting is in progress, but if it looks as if you will have to cut away much vegetation in order to obtain a clear view, find another nest. Exposing a nest lays it open to predators, so even if the parents tolerate the disturbance, it may ultimately fail. The nest must also be at the correct stage of development. Ideally the hide should not be introduced until after the eggs have hatched, partly because the best photo opportunities occur from this point onwards, and partly because this is when the parents' bond

I came upon this curlew's nest almost by chance while I was photographing a small colony of common gulls, the curlew landed nearby and moved warily through the heather to the nest. I began the process of moving the hide in right away, initially setting it up at thirty metres, and moving it closer each day. After a few days, the hide was five metres from the nest, and I crept in before sunrise the next morning. To my delight, the eggs were already beginning to hatch, and the first chick had emerged by mid morning.
300mm lens.

A hen eider on the nest.
300mm lens.

*Great crested grebe
displaying over the nest.*
400mm lens.

*Nest photography need not
always involve hackneyed
'bird feeding chick' shots.
Here, Russell was content to
photograph the robin as it
paused in the empty window
frame of the old shed in
which it had made its nest.
The result is appealing and
original. 300mm lens.*

with the nest is at its strongest. If you start before the eggs
have hatched, there is a greater risk of desertion. In the
case of species whose young leave the nest immediately
after hatching, there is no option but to begin during
incubation and proceed with caution. Initially the hide
should be set up well away from the nest, before being
moved progressively closer over a period of days. Exactly
how far away you should start depends on the sensitivity of
the species in question. While some garden birds will
accept the sudden appearance of a hide only 4 or 5m away,
as a general rule, 30m is a better starting point. At 24-hour
intervals, move the hide in, first to about 20m then 12m,
7m and finally your shooting distance of say, 4m. As you
close in on the nest, be particularly careful. After erecting
the hide, retreat to a discreet distance and observe the nest
to make sure that the parents are still coming and going as
normal. If the hide appears to be deterring them, it must
be moved back, but as long as you have not rushed the
procedure, it is likely that all will be well, and within a few
days of getting started you will be ready to begin shooting.

The process of acclimatising nesting birds to the hide will
be different if the nest is situated at such a height that the
hide must be erected on a tower. If the nest is in a hedge,

less than 2m above the hide's normal viewing level. there should be no problem, as a simple raised platform will do the job. This can be built from wooden boards and steel angle shelving supports such as Dexion. Although cumbersome, this type of platform can be dragged along when you wish to move it. Problems arise with nests higher than about 3m, as these require the use of a scaffold tower. Any tower too large to be dragged or carried over rough ground must be built from scratch in its final position. Erect it in stages, adding a section each day until the required height is reached. The hide can also be built in stages, 'growing' from innocuous beginnings to its full size by means of a couple of makeshift wooden frames.

When the time comes to begin taking pictures, enter and leave the hide discreetly, ideally when both parents are absent. If this is not possible, you'll need one or more accomplices to put you in and take you out. At all times, bear in mind that the birds' breeding success is at stake.

PHOTOGRAPHING BIRDS IN FLIGHT

Few subjects are as difficult to photograph as birds in flight. Slick camera handling skills are required; you must be able to compose, focus and shoot quickly and

A lapwing prepares to settle on perfectly camouflaged eggs. As with the curlew, the hide had to be set up well in advance of the eggs hatching, as the young leave the nest almost immediately. 300mm lens.

A home-made wooden hide raised up on a platform made from dexion shelving supports.

Another example of how the subjects' surroundings can make a shot. Herring gulls are hardly exotic subjects, and I was unable to get close enough to get them any larger in the frame. However, the lichens and sea pinks growing in the cliff below them were almost worthy of a picture in their own right, so I simply made the gulls the focal point of a wider scene.
500mm lens.

accurately. Furthermore, you must find (or engineer) a situation in which you can get close enough to the birds to obtain a worthwhile image with a lens of relatively moderate focal length, as it is difficult track birds in flight using an outsize super-telephoto. It's also important to have freedom of movement and a wide field of view, so ideally you shouldn't have to shoot from a hide.

Flight photography need not involve exotic equipment, unless you intend to rely on autofocus, in which case I would only recommend the top professionally specified cameras such as the Canon EOS1n and EOS 3, and the Nikon F5 and F100. When combined with the latest motorised lenses, these cameras are capable of outstanding autofocus performance. If you intend to use a manual focus outfit, the main consideration is simply that the lens should offer

sufficient reach while remaining small and light enough to handle easily. For once, here is a situation in which a fairly moderate focal length with a modest maximum aperture will out perform an expensive fast super-telephoto. My favourite lens for flight photography is a 300mm f/4. I've also done well with 180mm and 200mm lenses, but bear in mind that the shorter focal lengths have a wider field of view, so there is more chance of picking up a crooked horizon in the lower part of the frame. (I would defy anyone, when panning with a flying bird and concentrating on its placement within the frame, to simultaneously focus and check that the horizon is level before shooting!)

There is one piece of special equipment that can be a boon when attempting flight photography. This is the shoulder pod, which tucks into your shoulder to steady a hand-held camera. I use one of these in preference to a tripod, because it combats camera shake but allows more freedom of movement.

Because flight photography is a demanding technique, it's wise to pick an easy subject for your first attempts. The ideal subject would be large, slow flying, and approachable. Such obliging subjects do exist; as I've

When there is a good breeze coming in off the sea, gannets spend long periods hanging on the updraught. At times they become almost motionless, offering outstanding opportunities for flight photography.
180mm lens.

Russell employing a shoulder pod to steady his 180mm lens while photographing gannets as they wheel over the Bass rock.

Mind your head! The image of a swooping common tern will seem familiar to anyone who has wandered close to a nest. 35-105mm lens.

already mentioned, gannets are probably the best flight subjects you will ever encounter, and various other seabirds, notably fulmars, also provide good opportunities. Fulmars spend a lot of time making short flights around the immediate vicinity of the nest, swooping out from their ledges and then turning back in to skirt the cliff. Occasionally they too ride the updraught, sometimes venturing within a few feet of human observers when doing so.

Prior observation should help you to make sense of what might at first appear to be aerial chaos. It will become clear that most of the birds are following discernible flight paths. Having identified one, try to find a viewpoint which enables you to shoot from a favourable angle. Certain aerial 'poses' are more successful than others, and it's a basic requirement of any flight shot that the bird's wings be shown to good effect. A head-on viewpoint shows only the leading edge of the wing, unless you catch the start of a powerful downstroke, so that the wings are curving dramatically under stress with the primary feathers splayed. If you shoot directly from one side, so as to capture the bird's profile, the wing position also makes or breaks the shot. (If the near wing happens to point straight

at the camera, you get a picture of a flying torso!) The background is equally important. Try not to shoot against a blank overcast sky as this will appear on film as an unsightly white void. A confused background, such as an out of focus, sunlit cliff face, with its contrasting areas of light and shade, is also likely to produce an undesirable effect. Finally, beware of the seaward horizon, which will let everyone know whether the camera was level. Once you have found a suitable viewpoint, you should then be able to settle down and enjoy repeated photo opportunities as the birds sail past time and again along roughly the same line.

Most of the difficulties which arise in bird photography relate to fieldcraft. Advanced photographic techniques are usually less important than an understanding of the subject and the ability to get close to it. However, to succeed with birds in flight, you must handle the camera with some skill, particularly when focusing manually. The simplest manual technique is prefocusing. This involves focusing on a predetermined point ahead of an approaching subject, and allowing it to fly into focus. Two points are critical to success.

A pair of gannets sail on stiff wings over the Bass rock. Russell employed a different focusing technique for this than that used for the gannet hanging on the updraught. Because these subjects were moving rapidly toward the camera, he pre-focused ahead of the birds, kept them centre-frame as they approached, and fired the shutter a fraction of a second before they came into sharp focus. 180mm lens.

In contrast to gannets, puffins are small and fast flying and therefore make very difficult subjects for flight photography. The best opportunities occur as they brake just prior to touching down; capturing a profile like this is a real challenge. 300mm lens.

First, you must prefocus at the correct distance, so that when the subject pops into focus, it is also the right size within the frame. Second, your timing must be perfect, so as to catch the subject during the fraction of a second when it is truly sharp. If you wait until it looks sharp in the viewfinder, you've missed the shot. Instead, you must pan with the incoming subject (which initially will be well out of focus) and release the shutter fractionally before it appears sharp. Some practice will be required before you achieve an acceptable success rate, and a rapid motordrive will help. Long bursts of motordrive are counterproductive, because the viewfinder image is interrupted each time the mirror flips up and you will find it difficult to pan accurately. Try squeezing off short bursts of about three frames, spanning the moment when the subject passes through the point of focus; this can be very successful.

Although prefocusing is the most reliable manual focus technique, it's rarely possible to obtain more than one sharp frame at each attempt. With practice, and with a suitable subject, it is possible to adapt the normal manual focusing technique that you would use for a static subject, whereby the point of focus is progressively readjusted until

*Photographing wild raptors
in the air is difficult as you
are dealing with solitary
birds which, unlike many
seabirds, don't follow a
predictable flight path.
This red kite was attracted
by regular baiting, and was
photographed as it overflew
the area in front of the hide.*
600mm lens.

the image looks sharp. This method works best when shooting slow moving birds (again, gannets riding the updraught are a perfect example), as you need only contend with comparatively minor movements. It's less effective if the subject is approaching rapidly. Although a skilled photographer can repeatedly refocus to obtain several shots, it's unlikely that the subject will be the ideal size within the frame in more than one of them, so the overall success rate doesn't really exceed that of the simpler prefocusing technique.

Bear in mind that regardless of how accurate your focusing may be, a sharp result also depends on the shutter speed being used. The larger the subject within the frame, and the faster its movements, the faster the shutter speed must be. Generally it's best to shoot at 1/500s or faster. This requires good light, and often means using the lens wide open, which minimises the depth-of-field and makes accurate focusing all the more critical. Of course, there is no need to use fast shutter speeds if you wish to blur the subject deliberately and convey an impression of movement. In which case exposures as slow as 1s can be used.

*Strong backlighting and a
rich blue backdrop help to
bring out the feather pattern
in the wings of a herring gull.
Fast shutter speeds – 1/500
sec minimum – are required
if you wish to see this
kind of detail.*

While seabird colonies offer the best opportunities for flight photography, few of us have ready access to one, and in any case, these great gatherings are strictly seasonal events. Wildfowl can make good flight subjects all year round. To some extent the favourable conditions which prevail in seabird colonies also exist at park lakes. Here also, you have abundant, active, accessible subjects. Swans and geese make the easiest individual targets, particularly if you can capture a spectacular landing or take-off. In wetland areas, large flocks of wildfowl can make particularly dramatic images. I love evocative images that show flocks of geese or wader traversing a great expanse of sky and marsh. This type of shot should be treated as a 'landscape with birds'. Good composition is essential, so if possible, compose the shot before the birds appear, and just let them fly into the frame. This will ensure that you have a level horizon, and the right proportion of land, water and sky in the picture. The best chance to try this comes at sunset, with flocks of geese flying in to known roosts. From a suitable viewpoint, you can silhouette incoming flocks against the sunset .

Don't be disheartened if your success rate with flight shots seems low. Even seasoned professionals have a hard time making technically perfect, aesthetically pleasing images of birds in flight – which only makes a successful result all the more satisfying.

One of the more frustrating aspects of photography on many bird islands is that the boat drops you for a few hours only during the middle part of the day, so it's impossible to exploit the moody light of dusk and dawn. However, you can stay on some islands, such as the Isle of May, Handa and Skokholm, for up to a week. Weather permitting, you can then follow the old rule of thumb, "shoot early, shoot late". Malcolm captured this puffin silhouette during a week's stay on Skokholm. 600mm lens.

One dull and blustery March morning found us touring Islay, photographing barnacle geese from the car window. Poor light made flight photography difficult, but by shooting straight at the brightest part of the sunrise it was possible to obtain a workable shutter speed. We pulled up beside a flock that were obviously ready to fly – heads up, lots of warning honks and wary sideways looks as they waddled away. There was just time to focus before the flock lifted off; I raised the camera to frame the bright patch of sky, and fired a short burst of motordrive as these birds flew across the frame. 300mm lens.

STALKING WITH A CAMERA

The first image conjured up by the term 'stalking' is that of a heavily camouflaged photographer, lying prone in the undergrowth, and inching, Hiawatha-like, towards his or her unsuspecting quarry In reality, birds have such extraordinary eyesight that this approach is only worth trying in favourable terrain, where long grass, rocks, a wall, a gulley, or some other form of cover can provide concealment until you are close enough. Camouflaged clothing should be worn, cheap army surplus gear being ideal because the heavyweight cotton material doesn't rustle and the large pockets are suitable for carrying film and gadgets. Make sure you disguise the two key features by which birds immediately identify man. Cover your face with a ski-mask, a face veil, or a piece of scrim net. The other giveaway, the upright human form, is best disguised by crawling on your stomach, but be warned that travelling any distance on your elbows is an exhausting business, especially with a camera and 600mm lens in the crook of your arm. Nothing attracts a bird's attention more than movement, so move slowly and freeze when your quarry looks in your direction. The critical point comes when you are finally close enough, especially if you must break cover in order to get a clear field of view. If at this

point your quarry suddenly comes alert and appears ready to go, you have the option of freezing once more in the hope that it will calm down, or, if you think its departure is now inevitable, grabbing a quick shot before it goes. Only with experience will you be able to judge which is the better choice.

An alternative form of stalking involves approaching to within camera range while remaining in plain view. This may seem an unlikely tactic, but it often works better than the Hiawatha method, especially with birds that are accustomed to a certain amount of human contact, in parks and around harbours, for example. Birds which live around people are used to normal human behaviour, but they soon smell a rat when when somebody starts behaving furtively. Anyone peeping around tree trunks or sneaking along on all fours is given a wide berth. A better ploy is to remain visible and move obliquely toward your quarry while feigning disinterest. Look away and allow long pauses for the birds to settle and grow used to your presence; basically, the stalk should be a leisurely zig zag, completely unlike the direct approach of a predator. As long as you take your time, it can be a highly effective technique.

To obtain this shot, Malcolm moved in a little at a time and remained prone, waiting for the adult moorhen to settle down. After a while, she relaxed enough to resume feeding her chick.
600mm lens.

This is an example of 'stalking' in the true sense of the word. Russell has crawled up to the pheasant on his stomach, using the long grass as cover. There is often a lot of physical effort involved in this approach, but the shot gains considerably from the low viewpoint, and from the fact that it captures that moment when photographer and subject suddenly find themselves eye-to-eye.
500mm lens.

I noticed this moorhen making regular forays along the line of flag iris close to its nest. I crept into position while it was hidden from view. When it emerged, I remained motionless until it had worked its way along to this point, where the reflections would enhance the shot. 300mm lens.

Don't rely on stalking too much if you are hoping to consistently shoot frame filling portraits of individual birds. Neither of the techniques described above is a substitute for a well placed hide.

BIRDS IN CAPTIVITY

This book is essentially a guide to photographing wild birds in the field. However, not everyone has access to a salt marsh, an expanse of moorland, or even a back garden, and of those who do, most would accept that they have only a slim chance of photographing say, a wild peregrine. In recognition of this, it seems appropriate to cover techniques for photographing birds in captivity.

Mallards are the most ubiquitous of ducks, but there's no telling how difficult they may be to approach. In some public parks, they will take bread from your hand, whereas truly wild mallard are almost impossible to photograph unless you employ a hide. This bird fell between the two extremes, refusing to come closer than about five metres when tempted with bread. After some time though, Russell was able to move close enough for this portrait. 500mm lens.

Photographic magazines often carry articles on zoo photography, and these usually include advice on how to shoot captive subjects in such a way that they do not appear to be confined. This would be the basic aim for most photographers, but in my experience, it's almost impossible to achieve a convincing result just by following the stock advice of using a large aperture and getting close to the steel mesh so that it doesn't appear on film. Aviary birds tend to lurk up in some dark corner, posing forlornly in front of a nest box. For this reason I'd suggest that you concentrate on a zoo or wildlife park where at least some of the birds are not confined in enclosures. This should mean that your view is not obstructed by wire mesh and it may also be possible to shoot against a reasonably natural background. Falconry centres often display raptors in the

Falconry centres usually offer better photo opportunities than zoos, because the birds are often displayed in the open. Your view is not obstructed by wire mesh, and the lighting should be better. This Lanner falcon was photographed as I sat among the audience at a flying display. 400mm lens.

open. You may be able to move around them in order to shoot from the best possible viewpoint, but all the birds will be wearing jesses, and those used in flying displays may also be fitted with radio tracking aerials. (This is why you see so many head-and-shoulders portraits of captive raptors!) Of course, not every shot has to appear to have been taken in the wild, especially if you have the picture's commercial potential in mind; after all, there is a market for falconry subjects.

The best opportunities to shoot convincing images of captive birds occur if you can enlist the aid of a co-operative private owner. Often such an enthusiast will be keen to have some high quality prints of his or her birds, and will help you to set up some exceptional shots. Malcolm shot a series of barn owl portraits for this book using a bird whose owner kindly agreed to bring it out on location to a local farm. He also agreed to remove its jesses, but for security's sake, nylon fishing line was tied to the

This portrait of a tawny eagle benefits from the rimlighting effect achieved by shooting into the light. The head stands out against the dull background. 60-300mm lens.

Most captive birds become used to close contact with humans, so their natural behaviour is not inhibited by the presence of a nearby photographer. Russell settled down close to a captive Ruff, and eventually obtained this dramatic shot of the bird bathing. 500mm lens.

A different approach to photographing captive birds involves placing them in an authentic-looking environment to achieve a more natural effect. This barn owl was photographed with the assistance its owner. He agreed to bring the bird out to a farmyard, and to remove its jesses prior to each shot. 300mm lens.

ring on the owl's leg. This was kept hidden during shooting, and some excellent images resulted, as Malcolm was able to place the bird more or less where he liked and shoot from very close range using the short end of a 35-70mm zoom lens. The first session did end prematurely when the owl decided he'd had enough and nipped through the nylon line. To the consternation of his owner, he then flew into an open fronted barn and took refuge up in the rafters, where he remained until he was recaptured two hours later. Thereafter, the fishing line was replaced with fine wire.

When you are photographing a captive bird in a prepared setting, you have an exceptional degree of control over the final result. It should be possible to schedule the shoot for a day and time when the weather and lighting conditions are at their best. Visualise a series of 'ideal' images and plan the shoot around them. For once you can pick the ideal viewpoint, and move in close using a range of lenses. There should also be plenty of time to perfect the focus and composition. But as with any form of wildlife photography, your subject's well-being comes first, so if it becomes agitated, bring the session to a close.

Scarlet Ibis. Aviaries also offer the chance to photograph exotic species that would otherwise require a very expensive field trip! Again, the viewpoint was carefully chosen, so that the background appeared as natural as possible.
300mm lens.

Opposite: Soft natural lighting is ideal for close portraits like this one of a captive tawny owl.
300mm lens.

CONTROLLING EXPOSURE

Setting the exposure is a fundamental part of the picture-taking process. It involves selecting the most appropriate combination of lens aperture and shutter speed, the basic aim being to ensure that the correct amount of light reaches the film, so that the image is neither overexposed (too light) nor underexposed (too dark). The exposure controls can also be used to influence the 'look' of the photograph in other, more subtle ways. By varying the aperture setting, you can alter the depth of field, and by varying the shutter speed, you can alter the way in which movement is portrayed. Therefore, setting the exposure is both a technical procedure and a part of the creative process. This is why you should control it, rather than depend on a programmed camera. Clever electronics are no substitute for your creative input.

The basic principles of exposure are not difficult to master. The camera and lens between them offer two controls. One is the iris diaphragm of the lens (commonly known as the aperture), whose variable size regulates the volume of light entering the camera. The other is the camera's shutter, which can fire at different speeds in order to regulate the duration of the exposure. In order to control the exposure with enough precision, photographers

Left: This avocet's white breast would fool a light meter. The meter, being calibrated to produce an accurate result when directed at a middle tone, would interpret the lighter tone as more light. If you followed its recommendation, the shot would be grossly under exposed. Russell set this exposure in accordance with a reading taken from a middle tone in the background. Because he was dealing with a pure white subject, he then closed down the aperture by another half stop. This cut down the glare from the birds breast, ensuring that the plumage detail was retained.
500mm lens.

Right: Here the frame is dominated by the dark tones of the blackbird and the surrounding yew foliage. In order to make an accurate exposure, Russell took a light reading from a grey card that had been placed in the same light as the subject.
500mm lens.

measure light intensity in units called 'stops'. The scale of lens aperture settings and the range of shutter speeds are therefore graduated in stops, each stop representing a doubling (or halving, if you are working the other way) of the light intensity reaching the film.

Lens aperture settings are denoted by f-numbers, which might at first appear rather mystifying. Here is the aperture scale from my 300mm lens, beginning with the largest aperture:

f/4, f/5.6, f/8, f/11, f/16, f/22.

Why the odd progression of numbers – and how come the larger the aperture. the smaller the f-number? The answers lie in the fact that the f-number is arrived at by dividing the focal length of the lens by the diameter of the aperture in question. So, with the 300mm lens, f/4 denotes an aperture 75mm in diameter. Not that you need to know this in order to make an accurate exposure; just remember that the scale progresses in increments of one stop, and that the following principle applies:

small f-no. = large aperture = more light entering camera

Or, conversely:

large f-no. = small aperture = less light entering camera

Here the subject itself was the reference for the light reading. Russell spot metered the cormorant's back.
500mm lens.

Nature is full of middle-tones which can provide reliable references for exposure readings. One is a clear blue northern sky. All Russell had to do here was take a spot meter reading from the sky above the robin. 500mm lens.

Shutter speeds are measured in seconds, or fractions thereof. Some current SLRs allow you to set shutter speeds ranging from 30s (more useful to astronomers than bird photographers!) right up to an action-stopping 1/8000s. The following range includes the speeds that you are most likely to use when photographing birds with a medium speed film:

1/2s, 1/4, 1/8, 1/15, 1/30, 1/60, 1/125, 1/250, 1/500, 1/1000, 1/2000.

Again, the scale progresses in increments of one stop, a one-stop change in shutter speed affecting the exposure to the same extent as would a one-stop change in aperture. This means that any adjustment which is made to one control can be offset by making an equivalent (but opposite) adjustment to the other. As we'll see shortly, this an important point.

OBTAINING AN ACCURATE LIGHT READING

Of course, you can't just pick a random combination of aperture and shutter speed; the exposure must be set in accordance with the intensity of available light. Therefore, it's essential to obtain an accurate light reading.

Photographers measure light intensity with two basic types of light meter. One is the hand-held ambient light meter, which measures the ambient light level directly, responding to the intensity of the light falling upon it from the sky. It is reliable and simple to use, and remains 'standard kit' for many professional photographers. Its one drawback becomes apparent when the intensity of light falling on the meter is different from that falling on the subject. For example, you might be in shadow, while the bird you wish to photograph is in full sunlight. Unless you can move the meter into the same light as the bird (which may be impossible), you can't get an accurate reading. This is where the reflected light meter comes in. Some hand-held meters can take reflected light readings, but you might as well use the one that is built into your camera. This measures the intensity of the light being reflected by whatever is framed within the viewfinder, and the accuracy

In this shot, the priority was to expose for the background, as the geese were to be silhouettes. A spot meter is invaluable in this situation; all you need do is direct it at a portion of the sky which you judge to be middle toned. Absolute precision is rarely necessary with sunsets, because minor variations in exposure are unlikely to ruin the shot. Instead, they simply produce a change in mood. Nevertheless, its wise to bracket a little, if only to yourself a choice of different results; and when in doubt, err on the side of underexposure. 300mm lens.

A herring gull touching down at sunset. This shot is all about atmosphere, which is why the gull is simply the focal point of a wider scene. Because the subject need only be rendered as a virtual silhouette, it was possible to use an exposure which muted the glare of the sun, and emphasised the gathering gloom in the surrounding sky. 180mm lens.

of the reading depends on the tone of the surface being metered. Light-coloured surfaces naturally reflect more light than dark ones, so under the same illumination, different tones produce different readings. The best way to guarantee accuracy is to aim the meter at a middle-tone, or in other words, anything that is the equivalent of 18% grey. (All camera manufacturers calibrate their light meters to this tone.) Middle-tones are commonplace in nature. Examples include fresh green grass, most deciduous tree foliage, and, during the middle of the day, a clear blue northern sky. There are even plenty of middle-toned birds; just think of all those 'little brown jobs'! Because a certain amount of experience is required to judge tone accurately, I'd recommend that to begin with, you refer to a purpose-made photographer's grey card. Compare sample meter readings taken from various natural surfaces with readings taken from the grey card under the same illumination. Think in stops, saying to yourself, 'that dead grass is one-and-a-half stops lighter than the middle-tone', 'that yew foliage is one stop darker' and so on. Soon you'll be able to judge tonality without referring to the grey card.

In most cases, a meter reading taken from a middle-tone will guarantee an accurate exposure, regardless of the tone of the subject. The one exception arises when the subject is white. Pure white is so reflective that it may appear over exposed even though everything else in the picture is exposed perfectly. The only solution to this problem is to underexpose. In full sunlight, a white subject such as a swan should be given one stop less exposure than normal, so if you've selected an aperture of say, f/5.6, and a meter reading taken from a middle-tone indicates a shutter speed of 1/500s, you should actually set 1/1000s. Under more subdued lighting, no more than half a stop of underexposure will be required.

A male eider displays, apparently unaware of the photographer lying among rocks just a few metres away.
500mm lens.

SELECTING THE RIGHT COMBINATION OF APERTURE AND SHUTTER SPEED

Earlier, in discussing the relationship between aperture and shutter speed, I drew attention to the fact that when an adjustment is made to the aperture setting, it can be offset by making an equivalent adjustment to the shutter speed, and vice versa. This is significant because it means that from your meter reading, you can extrapolate a whole range of equivalent exposures, any of which could be used.

With the entire frame more or less middle toned, there were no exposure difficulties with this pheasant.
The camera's auto exposure modes will work perfectly in this situation. 500mm lens.

For example, imagine you've set the lens to its maximum aperture – say, f/4. When you meter a middle tone, the camera recommends a shutter speed of 1/1000 s. You aren't restricted to using 1/1000s and f/4; the same amount of light would reach the film if you used any one of the following exposures:

1/1000s at f/4; 1/500 at f5.6; 1/250 at f/8; 1/125 at f/11; 1/60 at f16; 1/30 at f/22.

In order to decide which is the most appropriate, consider how you want the picture to look, bearing in mind the effect of shutter speed on the portrayal of movement, and the effect of aperture size on the depth of field.

Assuming that the lens is accurately focused, the sharpness of the image depends on how much movement occurs during the exposure. The faster the shutter speed, the less potential there is for any movement to occur. For example, during a half second exposure, any discernible movement within the frame will be recorded as a blur, whereas a very brief exposure of 1/1000s will 'freeze' even rapid movements, guaranteeing a sharp image. So, if you are striving to obtain sharp images of a fast-moving subject, you should opt for the fastest possible shutter speed. Of

The grass in the foreground made a useful middle toned reference. Malcolm spot metered this area to obtain an accurate reading for the fulmar pair. 300mm lens

the range of exposures shown above, 1/1000s at f/4 would be the obvious choice.

In some situations, the depth of field is the main consideration. This is the area of the picture which appears to be sharp, and it extends before and beyond the exact point of focus. With the lens aperture set wide open (i.e. at the smallest f-number) the depth of field is at its most shallow – exactly as you see it in the viewfinder. However, as the lens is stopped down to the smaller aperture settings, the depth of field increases. (The increase can only be seen in the viewfinder if your camera has a depth of field preview facility.) One example of a shot which requires plenty of depth of field would be the classic wideangle portrait of a sitting seabird, featuring a sweep of coastal landscape as a backdrop. Ideally, both subject and background should be sharp. With a relatively static subject like this, a super-fast shutter speed is unnecessary, so you can afford to close down the aperture by several stops to obtain more depth-of-field. Referring to the example again, 1/125s at f/11 would be a good choice.

The creative potential of your camera's exposure controls does not stop here. While convention has it that a fast shutter speed should be used to 'freeze' a moving subject, you may prefer to convey an impression of movement by deliberately using shutter speeds as slow as 1s. This technique can produce artful images, but some experience and skill is required. Don't imagine that just because a picture is blurred, it must be artistic!

While I was photographing Canada geese on a local park lake, I was startled by the sound of heavy wings beating the water. I looked up to see this aggressive mute swan bearing down on the geese. The shutter speed I had set for the geese – 1/250 second – proved just adequate to squeeze the movement of the cob and the spray he was raising.
300mm lens

SUMMARY

Here is the entire procedure which I normally use to set the exposure manually:

1 *Set the camera's exposure mode to manual, and its metering mode to spot or centre-weighted.*

2 *Set the aperture. If your main priority is to obtain the fastest possible shutter speed, set the aperture wide open. If your main priority is the depth of field, use your camera's depth of field preview facility to determine the most appropriate aperture.*

3 *Direct the meter at an area of middle-tone which is under the same illumination as the subject. If the subject is middle-toned, and large enough in the viewfinder, meter it directly.*

4 *Set whatever shutter is speed is recommended by the camera as it meters the middle tone.*

5 *Compose, focus and shoot.*

What if no middle tone is available to provide an accurate meter reading? I described earlier how you can teach yourself to judge tone accurately. If you know that something is say, one stop lighter than a middle-tone, meter it, then open up one stop. For example, if you've selected f/5.6, and the meter reading indicates a shutter speed of 1/250s, set 1/125s. Alternatively, set a shutter speed of 1/250s, but open up the aperture to f/4. If the area being metered is one stop darker than a middle tone, go down a stop. Instead of setting the indicated shutter speed of 1/250s, set 1/500s; or set 1/250s, but close down the aperture from f/5.6 to f/8. With practice, this procedure becomes second nature. Like changing gear when you are driving a car, it is simpler to execute than it is to describe.

Throughout this chapter, I've described how to control exposure using whole stops, purely to make the explanations simpler. But adjusting the exposure by one stop has a considerable effect, especially if you are using transparency film. Often, you'll need to make fine exposure adjustments of less than one stop. This may be done by setting traditional lens-mounted aperture control rings part way between marked f- numbers. Alternatively, some recent electronic SLRs allow you to adjust both aperture and shutter speed settings in 1/3 stop increments.

Here I spot-metered the middle toned fencepost to obtain an accurate exposure for the redshank. 500mm lens

In order to obtain the fastest possible shutter speed and 'freeze' most of the movement in this shot of a bathing barnacle goose, Russell set the lens aperture wide open. 500 mm lens

BASIC FLASH TECHNIQUES

Most of the images in this book were made with daylight only, reflecting the photographers' belief that as a rule, natural lighting effects are preferable to anything you can achieve with flash. Unfortunately though, you can't always rely on natural light, even during the middle of the day. Overcast winter days can be dull enough to make daylight photography almost impossible, except with very fast films that cannot record fine quality images – and even in bright conditions, problems may arise if the subject is backlit or partially shaded. With electronic flash equipment, you can keep shooting regardless of the lighting conditions.

Left: Flash photography is quite simple when there is no need to simulate daylight. For this tawny owl portrait, Malcolm set the camera's fastest synch speed of 1/250s and the smallest aperture that fell within the range of his two flashes. The black background that resulted is quite appropriate for a nocturnal subject.
70-210mm lens.

Right: The same owl, but here the aim was to give an impression of late evening. This shot was actually taken in daylight, at lunchtime on an overcast day. To achieve the desired effect, Malcolm set an exposure which would drastically underexpose the sky in the background and make it appear almost dark. The flashes have perfectly illuminated the subject, but do not affect the background because it is too distant.
70-210mm lens.

In order to use flash effectively, you need to understand the mechanics of a flash exposure. The most important point is this: when you trigger the shutter, the flash doesn't fire until after the shutter has opened, and it is quenched before the shutter closes*. So, as far as the flash illumination is concerned, the shutter speed is irrelevant. It may affect the amount of daylight that registers on film, but whether you select 30s or 1/250s, the flash exposure will be the same.

The flash exposure may be controlled by altering the aperture setting and/or the output of the flashgun. At this point, I should clarify that the output of an electronic flashgun is altered by varying the duration (but not the intensity) of the flash. This may be done automatically or manually.

*N.B: A few cameras are compatible with special flashguns that produce an extended burst of flash. The shutter opens and closes during the flash, so the flash exposure can be controlled like daylight – i.e., by varying the shutter speed as well as the aperture.

Above left: A male greenfinch, shot entirely with natural light.

Above right: The same set up, illuminated entirely with flash. Two units are placed to each side of the camera. The unpleasant black background is the result of the light intensity decreasing, and failing to illuminate anything beyond the subject.

Right: Still the same set up, and once again lit entirely with flash, except that here an artificial backdrop (i.e., a sheet of plywood!) has been introduced, and illuminated with a third flash. With even lighting throughout the shot, a more natural effect is obtained.

AUTOMATIC FLASH

The most basic form of automatic flash control utilises a small sensor located on the front face of the flash unit. When the flash fires the sensor monitors the amount of light being reflected back from the subject, and when enough light has been supplied to ensure an accurate exposure, the flash quenches itself. Automatic flash works with large subjects but the sensor's field of view is too wide to accurately monitor the light reflected by a small bird.

TTL FLASH

The most efficient form of automatic flash control is the through-the-lens, or TTL system. In principle this is similar to automatic flash, the critical difference being that the exposure is monitored not by a sensor in the flashgun, but by the camera's meter. As a result, the exposure is tailored for the area framed within the viewfinder. TTL flash works in most situations, and it's convenient. There is no need to run exposure tests, and unless you set the flash at the extreme of its range, you have a choice of apertures. Problems may occur if there are excessively light or dark tones in the subject or background, in which case you may need to input some exposure compensation.

MANUAL FLASH CONTROL

When you set a flashgun to fire manually, it discharges a fixed amount of light every time. A simple flashgun that just has a 'manual' button fires at full power. More advanced flashguns, featuring a stepped manual control, allow you to select lower power settings typically 1/2, 1/4 or 1/8 power. (Some units go as low as 1/64 full power). This makes them much more versatile.

GUIDE NUMBER CALCULATIONS

The output of a flash unit is indicated by its guide number (GN). This helps you to set accurate manual flash exposures, but even if you are using TTL flash, the GN is useful, as it gives you an idea of the flashgun's maximum range.

Divide the GN by the flash-to-subject distance (in metres) and you get the approximate aperture required for an accurate exposure. For example, let's say the flash has a guide number of 40 and the flash-to-subject distance is 5m.

P.H.

This is a typical multiple flash set-up for photographing small birds at a feeding station. The subject, attracted to the perch by the lure of a nearby feeder, is illuminated by the two main units placed above and to either side of the camera position. An artificial backdrop – in this case, a painted board – is placed behind the subject, and is illuminated by a third flash, triggered by a slave unit. Some trial and error is required to determine the relative positions of flashes, subject and backboard. The aim is to achieve a natural looking effect by ensuring that the subject and background receive equal

40 ÷ 5 = 8, so the correct aperture would be f/8. Alternatively, divide the GN by the f-number to confirm the correct flash-to-subject distance.

There are several points to be aware of with regard to guide numbers. The first is that the guide number applies to a particular film speed, generally ISO 100. If you use a faster or slower film, the guide number changes. With an ISO 50 film, it would halve from say, GN40 to GN20. With an ISO 200 film, it would double to GN80. Guide numbers should be regarded as approximate if you are shooting outdoors. Usually they are based on the unit's indoor performance, where ceilings and walls bounce some extra light back at the subject. To determine your flashgun's true outdoor guide number, run some exposure tests. Set up a test subject (a small teddy bear is as good as anything) and shoot a series of exposures on transparency film, varying the lens aperture and/or flash-to-subject distance. Prior to making each exposure, write these details on a small card, and fix it to the test subject, so that they can be confirmed when you are examining the resulting transparencies.

If you use two flash units, you must combine their guide numbers when making exposure calculations. This is simplest if both flashes have the same output and are placed at the same distance from the subject; the total output of two GN40 units is then equivalent GN80. To calculate the correct aperture using flashes of differing output, placed at different distances from the subject, it's easier to work out the f-number for each flash separately, then add these two f-numbers together. For example, let's say we have one GN40 flash at 5 metres. 40 ÷ 5 = 8, so the correct aperture for use with this unit alone would be f /8. The second flashgun is rated at GN32 and is 4 metres from the subject. 32 ÷ 4 = 8, so the correct aperture for this unit alone would also be f /8. Add together the two f-numbers, and you get 16. The correct aperture when using these two flashes at these flash-to-subject distances is f/16.

If the prospect of having to run exposure tests and measure out flash-to-subject distances etc. seems tiresome, bear in mind that once the correct exposure is arrived at, it works for any subject and background.

AVOIDING BLACK BACKGROUNDS

One of the most unsightly features that can appear in a poorly executed flash exposure is the giveaway black background. While a black background may be appropriate for a nocturnal subject, it is unacceptable as a background for a diurnal bird.

Black backgrounds occur when whatever is behind the subject is too far from the flashgun(s) to receive sufficient illumination to register on film. A basic law of physics is responsible; the light decreases in intensity as it moves farther from its source. A simple guide number calculation illustrates this; GN40 gives you f/8 at 5m, or f/4 at 10m. In other words, for each doubling in distance, two stops of light are lost. How then can you overcome this problem? One solution is to decrease the shutter speed and/or open the aperture go that the background is illuminated by daylight. However, by mixing flash and daylight in this way, you introduce the risk of a 'ghost' image appearing, should the subject move during the exposure (As soon as the shutter opens, the flash fires, making a sharp image; this is then is overlaid by a blurred daylight image, made in the interval between the flash being quenched and and the closure of the shutter). The other solution is only feasible if you can bring the birds into a prepared environment – in effect, an unenclosed studio. This is quite possible at a garden feeding station, for example. First, set up an artificial backdrop, such as a cloth screen or a painted board. This can be placed just behind the subject so as to

This captive-bred tawny owl chick was placed in the fork of a dead tree trunk and photographed with flash. The effect is of a wild bird photographed at night.
70-210mm lens.

be illuminated by the main light source(s), but ideally, it should be farther back, so that there is no risk of the subject casting a giveaway shadow on it. Another advantage of placing the backdrop well beyond the subject is that it will be well out of focus. However, it will have to be illuminated by an additional flashgun. Triggering a relatively distant flashgun is best done with a slave unit. This is a small, inexpensive gadget that connects to any flash unit via a standard hotshoe, and it is sensitive to sudden bursts of light. It triggers the attached flashgun whenever another is fired nearby. Because automatic control of the slave flash's output is not possible, you should run exposure tests, varying the flash-to-backdrop distance. You should find that, depending on the film speed and aperture being used, a small GN20 unit will do the job from 2-3m.

FILL-IN FLASH

In addition to saving the day when light levels fall too low to allow daylight exposures, flash can solve more subtle lighting difficulties, such as those which arise when you encounter a shaded subject against a sunlit background. In this situation, exposing for the subject results in a grossly overexposed background. Conversely, exposing for the background causes the subject to appear as little more than a silhouette. The solution is to even up the lighting by filling in the shaded area with a moderate burst of flash.

Modern cameras simplify fill-in flash considerably. Generally, the camera's evaluative metering system will do an excellent job of balancing flash and daylight, although you may need to dial in some exposure compensation for a particularly light or dark subject. Owners of older, less sophisticated cameras, will have to use the traditional method. First, set an aperture one stop smaller than that indicated by the GN of the flash. For example, if the flash has a true GN of 40, and you are shooting from 5m, set f/11 rather than f /8. Then meter a middle-tone in the most brightly lit part of the frame, and set whatever shutter speed is indicated. Now you can shoot. But what if you meter the bright area, and the meter indicates a shutter speed that exceeds the maximum synch speed of the camera? In this case you must use a smaller aperture so as to get a slower shutter speed. As a consequence of using a smaller aperture, you'll need more flash illumination for the subject, so you must either move the flash closer (a guide number calculation, based on the new aperture, will tell you how close it should be) or employ an additional flash.

Problems can arise when using fill-flash in poor light, because a slower shutter speed must be used, which once again introduces the risk of recording a 'ghost' daylight image. All you can really do in this situation is load a faster film, and accept some loss of image quality.

This robin made its nest in an old teapot that had been left among the ivy in a garden hedge. The gloomy location made flash an essential part of the set up. 80-200mm lens.

POSITIONING THE FLASHGUNS

The position of the flashgun(s) is critical. A single on-camera flash will produce the least desirable effect, with harsh shadows and possibly red-eye (light reflecting back off the bird's retina) ruining the shot. Two flashes will produce a more pleasing effect, especially when placed above and to each side of the camera. The result is even illumination, no unsightly shadows, and no red-eye. When flash is being used to photograph a nocturnal subject, an owl being the obvious example, the whole set up can be changed. Since you no longer have to simulate daylight, black backgrounds and deep shadows can be acceptable or even desirable. With practice more ambitious effects can be achieved. For example, by sidelighting the bird with the main flash and weakly illuminating the background from the same direction using a secondary unit, you can simulate moonlight quite convincingly.

THE CREATIVE APPROACH

Bird photography is apt to become a passion, and because dedicated bird photographers have been around for decades, there is hardly a species or an aspect of behaviour that has not been recorded on film. But don't imagine that it is no longer possible to do anything new. In spite of the species-orientated approach favoured by some, its not what you photograph that counts, but how you photograph it. I believe that the future of bird photography lies with creative individuals who treat it as an art form.

Some photographers continue to produce hackneyed record shots because they are hamstrung by the belief that first and foremost, a wildlife photograph should be a faithful representation of reality. In fact, no photograph can fulfil this requirement. When you look at a photograph, you see only what the photographer chose to include within the frame, and by selecting a certain viewpoint, lens, exposure setting, composition, and lighting effect. the photographer had ample scope to be economical with the truth. Also, whatever the photographer's intention, there are inescapable differences between the way we see things, and the way they are recorded on film. For example, when a bird flies overhead, we don't see every feather in its wing, as you can in a photograph made with a 1/1000s exposure. Nor do we see the wraith-like blur that results from a 1/2s exposure. Because our eyes focus on whatever we look at, we have no awareness of depth of field. We even see colour and the contrast between light and shadow quite differently from the way they are reproduced on film.

No-one can define exactly what it is that makes an image 'artful'. But artful images are invariably characterised by a sense of order. To make ordered images from the apparent chaos of nature you must train yourself to see in terms of line, form, colour and texture. Once you can do this (and you may discover a natural gift for it) you'll see the more subtle and unusual picture opportunities that other photographers miss.

Outstanding images have little to do with exotic subject matter, and everything to do with the originality of the photographer's approach. Pictures of mute swans are two a penny, but this is different. The viewpoint is an inch or so above water level, and was achieved by standing in the water at the foot of a weir, and shooting over the weir at the swan as it approached the camera head on. The shot is timed to catch the moment when he pushes up a bow wave as he surges forward. The composition places the subject high enough in the frame to also include its defocused reflection, and soft sunlight adds the finishing touch. This dramatic image was a category winner for Russell in the British Gas Wildlife Photographer of the Year competition.
500mm lens.

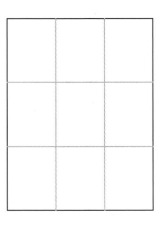

Further proof that ordinary subjects can become extraordinary given the right treatment. In this shot, warm sidelighting works wonders for the humble coot.
400mm lens.

The aesthetic appeal of a picture depends largely on its composition; here is an obvious manifestation of the sense of order I've just mentioned. Good composition is not a matter of getting the subject as large in the viewfinder as possible and placing it centre-frame. Such pictures do not hold the viewer's eye, because at a glance, you see all there is to see. If the subject is a little smaller in the frame, there is space around it for the viewer's eye to explore. The eye is further intrigued if the subject is placed at one of several key points within the frame. Artists use a couple of 'rules' which help to define these points, the best known among photographers being the 'rule of thirds', whereby the frame is divided into thirds, both vertically and horizontally. Try to mentally superimpose a grid of two

A rule of thirds grid.

There is a maxim in photography, 'shoot early, shoot late'. It refers to the quality of light that you encounter early and late in the day. This mute swan is glowing in last few minutes of sunlight on a summer's evening. 300mm lens.

vertical and two horizontal lines on to the frame. Each of the intersections of these lines represents a point of visual power. When the subject is placed on any one of these, the composition becomes more dynamic.

When composing with a bird on an off-centre placement, it's normally preferable to have it face into the frame, because the viewer's eye tends to follow the subject's line of sight, as if wanting to see where the subject is looking, or where it is going. The area behind the subject becomes dead space.

As a rule, composition should be kept simple, because simple pictures have more impact. As the saying goes, less is more. Some of the pictures in this book contain a bird, its perch, and nothing else. This sounds like a recipe for a pretty boring picture, but in fact, these shots work well. The subject dominates the frame and holds the viewer's eye because it is not competing with anything. Of course, not every picture should be simplified to this extent, but you should certainly try to exclude anything which is irrelevant to, or which distracts from, the visual message you wish to convey.

Your choice of viewpoint is critical. Generally I try to avoid shooting from the normal 'human's eye' viewpoint about 1.7m above the ground, particularly if the subject is on the ground or on water. In this situation, it's often preferable to get the camera as low as possible and shoot on the subject's eye level, or even lower. This gives the viewer a sense of intimacy with the subject, and visually it's refreshing to see the world from such an unfamiliar viewpoint. It also tends to produce a pleasing effect whereby the subject really 'pops' between the acutely de-focused foreground and background.

Lighting is important in determining the mood of a picture. I have a strong preference for natural lighting effects, which of course vary enormously depending on the time of day, time of year, and the weather. The quality of natural light ranges from the cool, even illumination of an overcast day, to the glare of the afternoon sun in July. Many experienced photographers dislike shooting in full sunlight, because although it allows you to use fast shutter speeds, it's very harsh and there is terrific contrast between areas of highlight and shadow, which can be problematic. Unlike the human eye, film cannot deal with extremes of light and shade, so when you expose for bright sunlight,

If you go out with your camera regularly enough, and especially if you get out really early, you'll find that nature can provide some beautiful filter effects. These Canada geese were photographed before the sun had begun to burn off the overnight mist. 500mm lens.

This image was made on the shore of Loch Indaal in Islay, at the end of a peaceful day in late March. Barnacle geese were flying in from all over the island to roost at the head of the loch, and this evocative shot was taken as the stragglers of a huge flock drifted down against the sunset. 35-70mm lens.

shadows appear black and unsightly. The low sunlight of early morning and evening is different; this produces a warm, mellow effect which no doubt inspired the photographic adage that says, 'shoot early, shoot late'. (In fact, on clear mid-winter days when the sun stays low, you can shoot in wonderful light all day. Most British photographers would agree that this is some compensation for the fact that, on the other nine days out of ten, it rains!) The diffused light of a cloudy day can be difficult to work with, because being less intense, it compels you to use slower shutter speeds. However, it can be flattering to subtle colours and the fine detail of close portraits.

In the section on exposure I described how, by using different combinations of shutter speed and aperture, you can portray a subject in different ways. Depth of field can be minimised to make the subject 'pop' against an out-of-focus background, or increased to give a better impression of the subject's surroundings. Fast action may be frozen to reveal detail that the human eye would not normally see, or deliberately blurred to achieve a more impressionist effect.

When a pair of robins nested in his garden shed, Russell moved a hide in but was careful to avoid repeating the usual hackneyed images of young birds clamouring for worms. His approach certainly succeeds here, thanks to the unusual setting and beautiful lighting.
180mm lens.

Another, more original alternative to the obvious image of a parent feeding chicks at the nest.
180mm lens.

The pose of these two young starlings adds a comic touch to the shot; it's a picture that invites a caption.
500mm lens.

CONCLUSION

Finally, I'd recommend using 'props' (as described in the section on photographing small birds at a feeding station) to impose a little more order than there might otherwise be. This is an excellent way of ensuring that you get just the composition, lighting and background that you require. Some photographers worry that this is cheating. Maybe so, but I would argue that nature makes things so hard for us bird photographers, that cheating a little just redresses the balance.

EQUIPMENT

Throughout this book, I've assumed that you'll be using using a 35mm SLR, because this type of camera is unquestionably the best tool for photographing wildlife in the field. From a bird photographer's point of view, its biggest advantage is its compatibility with a wide range of lenses, especially the super-telephotos required to produce frame-filling image of small, relatively distant subjects. In addition, 35 mm equipment is reasonably affordable, portable, and easy to use.

If you are new to photography, or out of touch with recent advances in photographic technology, you may find the sophistication of the latest electronic SLRs bewildering. Be assured that despite the manufacturers' hype, clever electronics have a comparatively minor role to play in the making of outstanding images. If your fieldcraft is lacking and you have no creative sense, no amount of technology will help you. On the other hand, if you are a competent photographer with a good 'feel' for your subject, you will produce fine work with even the most basic manual camera.

Provided a camera offers full manual exposure control and has a cable or remote release socket, it can do the job, although some additional refinements will make the job easier. These would include a depth of field preview button, spot metering, and a motordrive. In my opinion, autofocus is not essential, and as proof of this I would offer the fact that we focused manually to shoot every picture in this book. However, autofocus can be useful, especially if you can afford one of the latest professionally specified SLRs from Canon or Nikon. These feature superb AF performance which can be a boon for action and flight photography. Any additional electronic wizardry is superfluous.

In return for the time you spend on establishing hides, you get the opportunity to photograph shy birds like this grey heron from a really intimate viewpoint. Just being able to observe the birds this closely makes the effort worthwhile.

Of course, these days it's hard to find a camera that isn't over-specified, so by all means purchase an autofocus, multi-program, PC compatible, auto-bracketing SLR; just make sure that none of the automation interferes when you wish to use the camera in 'manual everything' mode.

LENSES

The quality of your pictures will be influenced far more by the quality of your lens than by the sophistication of your camera. The first point to consider with regard to lenses is focal length. This determines the lens's angle of view, and hence, how large the subject's image will appear when shot from a given distance. The greater the focal length, the larger the image. Most bird photographers rely on a super-telephoto of between 300mm and 600mm as a 'main' lens, employing shorter focal lengths when a tolerant subject allows an unusually close approach, or when it is desirable to picture the subject against a sweep of its environment.

If you are happy to do most of your photography from a hide, a 300mm makes a useful main lens. This is often the ideal focal length for nest photography, and for photographing small birds at a garden feeding station. It's also just right for capturing birds in flight, being compact enough to be hand-held or used on a shoulder pod for long periods. For car window photography, stalking, and other situations where you can't get close enough to shoot worthwhile images with a 300mm, a 400mm or 500mm is a good choice. However, don't get carried away with the idea that more focal length will solve all your problems. No matter how long your lens, there is always another great subject that could be photographed if only you had something longer! Rather than spend a fortune on a 600mm or 800mm lens, spend more time establishing hides and getting closer to the birds; this really brings results.

The lens's maximum aperture is as important as its focal length. The larger the aperture, the more light is transmitted to the film, so the faster the shutter speed you can use. A 'fast' lens (i.e. one with an exceptionally large maximum aperture) also produces a bright viewfinder image with a more distinct point of focus. Unfortunately, fast super-telephotos have to be large, heavy, and expensive. A 300mm f/2.8 costs about four times as much as a 300mm f/4, and won't bring about a major improvement in the quality of your pictures. That said, a really 'slow' lens can be a serious hindrance. Anything with a maximum aperture of f/8 or smaller is too slow, which is why I wouldn't consider a 500mm mirror lens.

The final question is whether to opt for a prime lens (i.e. a lens of fixed focal length) or a zoom. The variable focal length of a zoom lens enables you to vary the composition

Simple pictures usually work well. This shot derives its impact from the owl's strongest and most distinctive feature, its eyes. 105mm macro lens.

(and hence the size of the subject within the frame) without moving closer or farther away. This can be a great advantage, particularly when shooting from the fixed viewpoint of a hide. The main disadvantage with zooms is that most (though not all) are about one stop slower than the equivalent prime lens. For example, a typical 75-300mm zoom has a maximum aperture of f/5.6, whereas most 300mm prime lenses offer f/4.

Don't imagine that you need a vast array of lenses. One long lens of between 300mm and 500mm, backed up by one or two shorter lenses (say, a wideangle and a 70-210mm zoom) is a very versatile outfit. With regard to quality, buy the best you can afford, even if you must settle for a more basic camera body to do so. Fortunately there are now very few poor lenses around. All of the well known camera manufacturers produce superb optics, and the better 'independent' lenses, while marginally inferior, can still turn in professional results. But do avoid those cheap, obscure eastern European lenses; their front elements are made from jam-jar bottoms.

TRIPODS

A tripod is essential. Unless you use one, many of your hard-earned photo opportunities will come to nothing, as the image will be ruined by camera shake. A tripod is also the only means of supporting the camera, ready for immediate use, throughout a long hide session, and it allows you to frame a subject and maintain the desired composition for a whole series of exposures. Surprising then that so many photographers, many of whom regularly update their cameras at great expense (and see no improvement in their pictures as a result), will not invest in a good tripod. My advice is to do so, and to use it habitually. Look for a rugged, heavy design and make sure it can support the camera right up to your eye level when standing. It should not have a long centre column, because this restricts your legroom in a cramped hide. It also prevents you from positioning the camera close to ground level. One or two manufacturers offer short replacement centre columns; alternatively, you could do a conversion with a hacksaw, as I have done to my Benbo Mk2.

The tripod must be fitted with a head, of which there are three basic types: 3-way pan/tilt, ball, and video. If I were choosing a head purely for bird photography, I'd opt for a large ball head. Ball heads promote fast camera handling and the larger models like the Graf Studioball will support the heaviest lenses. Video heads, while beautifully smooth, cannot be 'flopped' to shoot in portrait format, an essential requirement when using any lens that lacks a rotating tripod collar. 3-way heads are excellent for general nature photography, but can slow you down somewhat when shooting fast action.

ACCESSORIES

A remote (or cable) release is indispensable, because It enables you to trigger a tripod-mounted camera without touching it, thereby eliminating any risk of camera shake blurring the picture.

A pair of powerful flash units will enable you to take pictures when poor lighting would otherwise make photography impossible. If you are prepared to conduct some exposure tests to confirm the units' exact power, manual-only units will prove adequate. TTL control, whereby the output of the flash is controlled automatically by the camera's computer, costs more but is a great convenience. If you are budgeting for a comprehensive flash outfit – ideally based on two identical units, each with a guide number of 40 or above – don't forget to include the cost of rechargeable power packs, chargers, remote leads, and possibly a couple of cheap tripods for supporting them off-camera. A smaller third flashgun and a slave unit will also come in handy.

Anyone who photographs small birds with a conventional prime lens will find a short extension tube (about 25mm in length) indispensable. An extension tube fits between camera and lens, and enables the lens to focus closer. Without one, many super-telephoto lenses cannot focus close enough to produce frame-filling images of small birds.

Another favourite accessory among long lens users is the teleconverter. Like an extension tube, this fits between camera and lens, but its function is to multiply the focal length of the lens. Teleconverters are available in various strengths. The only one I would recommend is the x1.4, which will convert, say, a 300mm lens into a 420mm; or a 400mm into a 560mm. The increase in focal length is accompanied by a reduction in the intensity of light reaching the film. In the case of the x1.4, one stop is lost, so an f/4 lens becomes an f/5.6. A good teleconverter costs almost as much as a good lens. Don't buy a cheap one unless you can tolerate a noticeable loss of image quality.

I use three types of filter. One is a circular polariser, which cuts down reflections from shiny surfaces to reveal the full richness of their underlying colour. Polarisers are particularly effective on clear skies, darkening them to a rich royal blue, but when used to maximum effect they steal a lot of light, so they can only be used when you can get away with moderate shutter speeds. Typically I use one on a short lens, when photographing immobile subjects in sunny conditions. My other filters, rarely used for birds are an 81B, which produces a subtle warming effect, and a graduated neutral density filter.

Two other items are worthy of inclusion. Each of your lenses should be fitted with a hood. This humble accessory can visibly improve image quality by reducing flare. This improves colour saturation and contrast, thereby enhancing the impression of sharpness. My final 'handy gadget' is a photographer's grey card, which serves as a reliable reference for reflected light readings, thereby helping you to make accurate manual exposures.

FILM

Three factors combine to determine the technical quality of a photographic image. These are the soundness of the photographer's technique, the quality of the lens, and the quality of the film upon which the image is recorded.

Most dedicated wildlife photographers shoot exclusively on colour transparency (slide) film. Transparency film is favoured for various reasons. For one thing, a transparency carries a first generation image, made in-camera. By contrast, a print is a second generation image. It cannot match the quality of the negative from which it is made. To be certain of obtaining perfectly exposed prints, you must do your own printing, or pay more money for hand printing. Transparencies have more commercial potential than prints; magazines, book publishers and agencies prefer them, and they can be stored for years without serious deterioration. Top quality prints can be made from transparencies, whereas top quality transparencies cannot be made from prints. Finally, should you wish to present illustrated talks to groups of fellow birders or photographers, a good slide show beats a collection of prints every time.

Film comes in a range of 'speeds'. Slow films – those with an ISO number of less than 100 – can record extremely sharp, grain-free images, but they dictate the use of slow shutter speeds. Faster films allow you to use faster shutter speeds but they exhibit more grain, which detracts from the impression of clarity and sharpness. The ideal film would be fast enough to permit the use of workable shutter speeds, but slow enough to record an acceptably grain-free image. Some photographers use several different films, loading whichever speed is best suited to the prevailing lighting conditions and subject. I prefer to keep things simple, and for 90% of my bird photography I get by with one 'all-round', medium-speed film. This is Fuji Sensia II in ISO 100. There are various other high quality ISO 100 films available, so try them and see which one you prefer. Sensia happens to be my favourite because it's remarkably sharp and I like its richly saturated colours. At ISO 100 it's viable in most situations, but if the light is poor it can, like any other E-6 film, be 'pushed', or exposed as though it were faster than its rated speed. (To do this, set the film speed to say, ISO 200, expose the whole roll at that setting, and notify the processor that you have done so.)

A yellowhammer basks in the last few moments of sunlight at the end of a clear day in mid-winter. 300mm lens with x1.6 teleconverter.

IN CONCLUSION

All of the images in this book were made using the techniques outlined in the text. If you use these same techniques, your pictures will be just as sharp and well exposed. Anyone can shoot razor sharp pictures if they fit a good lens to their camera, support it with a tripod or beanbag, and use slow to medium speed film. Mastering the principles of exposure is a little trickier, but if you use your camera regularly you'll soon become proficient. But technical excellence alone isn't enough. An outstanding picture must also have some aesthetic and emotional appeal, which is where your creativity comes in. Perhaps you are naturally gifted in this respect. If so, you have it made, but even if you don't think of yourself as particularly creative, be assured that you are still capable of producing pleasing work.

Here's the most important piece of advice so far: get out there and take pictures! Inexperienced photographers who shoot lots of film soon become experienced photographers. Persistent photographers get more and better pictures, and they are luckier – but only because they try harder, for example by staying an extra couple of hours in the hide on a freezing day, or by hiking the extra mile to the next cliff. Time and again, that bit of extra effort is rewarded.

Finally, I would re-emphasise that an over-zealous wildlife photographer can do considerable harm, especially by disturbing birds at the nest. Make your subject's welfare your first concern, and you'll derive more enjoyment from your art.

INDEX & PHOTO CREDITS

PHOTO CREDITS;

Malcolm Freeman – 2, 17, 20, 23, 25, 32, 33, 35, 44, 47, 49, 54, 60, 62, 64, 69, 70, 73, 82, 86, 87, 93, 99, 107, 111.

Russell Hartwell – 1, 8, 18, 21, 22, 24, 30, 34, 42, 43, 51, 52, 53, 56, 57, 58, 59, 61, 65, 67, 71, 72, 74, 75, 76, 77, 79, 80, 81, 85, 95, 96, 98, 100, 101, 102, 103, 104.

Paul Hicks – 6, 10, 11, 14, 15, 27, 29, 31, 36, 37, 38, 39, 40, 41, 45, 46, 48, 50, 55, 63, 66, 68, 78, 83, 84, 88, 89, drawings 12, 91.